BERSHEH
REPORTS I

BERSHEH REPORTS I

REPORT OF THE 1990 FIELD SEASON OF THE JOINT EXPEDITION OF THE

Museum of Fine Arts, Boston

University Museum, University of Pennsylvania

Leiden University

Edward Brovarski   Rita E. Freed   Olaf Kaper
Jean-Louis Lachevre   Melissa Robinson   David P. Silverman
René van Walsem   Harco Willems

MUSEUM OF FINE ARTS, BOSTON

1992

Cover: General view of tombs on the high terrace of the north side of the wadi at Deir el-Bersheh, looking west. Photograph by Rus Gant (RG 90/55–22).

Frontispiece: Interior of the tomb of Ahanakht (Tomb R 5/EEF 5). Photograph by Rus Gant (RG 90/57–37).

Back cover: Pathway and lower terrace tombs on the north side of the wadi at Deir el-Bersheh, looking north. Photograph by David P. Silverman (DPS 90/27–21).

Typeset in Palatino with special characters designed by Peter Der Manuelian

Hieroglyphic digital typeface designed by Cleo Huggins

Designed on an Apple Macintosh computer
and printed on a Linotronic 300 Imagesetter

Copyedited, designed, and produced by Peter Der Manuelian
Department of Ancient Egyptian, Nubian, and Near Eastern Art

ISBN 0–87846–365–8

Manufactured in the United States of America
by
Henry N. Sawyer Company
Charlestown, Massachusetts

CONTENTS

PREFACE ix
David P. Silverman

LIST OF FIGURES x

LIST OF ABBREVIATIONS xiii

CHAPTER I: THE BERSHEH NECROPOLIS 1
Melissa Robinson

A. Physical Description of the Site 3

B. History of Work at the Site 7

CHAPTER II: TOMBS AT THE EAST AND WEST ENDS OF THE HIGH TERRACE 11

A. Reisner 1– Nehri II 13

1. Physical Description 13
Melissa Robinson

2. Epigraphic Work 15
David P. Silverman

B. Reisner 7 (EEF 'M') 27
Edward Brovarski

C. Reisner 18 – Amenemhat 27
Edward Brovarski

D. Reisner 19 – Nehri I 28
Edward Brovarski

E. Reisner 21 – Djehutynakht 30

1. Physical Description 30
Melissa Robinson

2. Epigraphic Work 35
Edward Brovarski

CHAPTER III: TOMBS IN THE MIDDLE OF THE TERRACE 39

A. Introduction 41
René van Walsem and Harco Willems

B. Archaeological History 41
René van Walsem and Harco Willems

C. Tomb 5 – Ahanakht 43
Olaf Kaper

D. Tomb 102 – Iha . . . 47
René van Walsem

E. Tomb 104 – Djehutynakht . . . 48
Harco Willems

CHAPTER IV: ART HISTORICAL OVERVIEW . . . 51
Rita E. Freed

A. Introduction . . . 53

B. Tomb 5 – Ahanakht . . . 53

C. Tombs 102 & 104 – Iha & Djehutynakht . . . 59

D. Tomb 19 – Nehri I . . . 61

E. Tomb 1 – Nehri II . . . 62

F. Conclusions . . . 63

CHAPTER V: OTHER WORK . . . 65

A. Site Reconaissance . . . 67
Edward Brovarski

1. Lower Terrace . . . 67

a. Fraser's Tomb D (c): The Decree of King Neferefre . . . 67

2. South Side of the Wadi . . . 67

a. The Tomb of Ankhy . . . 67

b. The Tomb of Impy . . . 69

B. Mapping Project . . . 69
Melissa Robinson

C. Database Project . . . 70
Melissa Robinson

D. Conservation Report . . . 70
Jean-Louis Lachevre

BIBLIOGRAPHY . . . 73

PREFACE

The 1990 season of the Bersheh Expedition lasted from March 6–27. The expedition was jointly sponsored by the Museum of Fine Arts, Boston, the University Museum of the University of Pennsylvania, and Leiden University. The staff consisted of Edward Brovarski and Rita E. Freed (Boston), David Silverman (Philadelphia), René van Walsem and Harco Willems (Leiden), Co-Directors; Melissa Robinson, Assistant Director and Chief Epigrapher (Philadelphia); Rus Gant, Photographer (Boston); Olaf Kaper, Epigrapher and Coptologist (Leiden); Edward Gyllenhaal, Jennifer Houser, Brian Muhs, Epigraphers (Philadelphia); Jean-Louis Lachevre, Conservator (Boston). Hisham Hegazy served most competently as manager and assistant. The expedition received much interest and support from the two inspectors, Mr. Adel Makary (American) and Mr. Abdel Latif Ibrahim (Dutch).

The expedition was fortunate to have had the advice and encouragement of the late Dr. Sayed Tawfik, Chairman of the Egyptian Antiquities Organization, as well as the support and interest of Dr. Kamal Fahmy, Dr. Zahi Hawass and Dr. Abdel Aziz Sadek. Mr. Yehya Zakaria Mohamed, Chief Inspector of Antiquities at Mallawi, was extremely helpful throughout the 1990 season, and we are grateful to him and his staff for all the assistance they offered to our project. A special expression of gratitude is due Mr. Adel Hassan, Chief Inspector of Minia, who spared no effort on our behalf. We also thank Dr. Robert Betts, then Cairo Director of the American Research Center in Egypt, Mrs. Amira Khattab, Assistant to the Director, and Dr. Terry Walz, New York Director of the Center, for their help in many ways.

On the Boston side, the field work of the 1990 season was supported by generous contributions from the Vaughn Foundation Fund through Mr. and Mrs. James M. Vaughn Jr., from the Marilyn K. Simpson Charitable Trust, from Mr. and Mrs. Gorham L. Cross, Dr. René Gelman, Mr. and Mrs. Arnold Haynes, Dr. Paul Chapman, Dr. and Mrs. Robert P. Nebesar, and Mr. and Mrs. Richard Fraser. On the Pennsylvania side, we would like to thank Dr. Robert Dyson, Dr. David O'Connor, and the University Museum for supporting our work this season. We also wish to express appreciation for the generosity of Mr. and Mrs. Bruce Mainwaring, the Harrison Fund of the Museum, the Academy of the New Church in Bryn Athyn, Jack and Elsie Warner, and Melissa Robinson. Their interest in our behalf allowed us to meet our goals.

The work of the Dutch team would have been impossible without the financial support of the Netherlands Institute for Archaeology and Arabic Studies in Cairo, the Netherlands Institute for the Near East in Leiden, the Oosters Genootschap (Leiden), art gallery "Liga Nieuw Beelden" (Leiden), and of the Netherlands Organization for Scientific Research. We are also grateful to Margaret and Bruce Mauwaring and the Harrison Fund. Apart from these, Mr. G. Borg and his staff at the Netherlands Institute in Cairo welcomed and assisted the Dutch members of the expedition.

This report on our work at Bersheh has been made possible in part by a grant from the National Endowment for the Humanities. This funding has allowed the editors to prepare this volume expeditiously and to continue their research and recording for future seasons at Bersheh.

This manuscript represents the combined efforts of many talented individuals, both in the field and at home. Each of the senior staff members prepared a carefully executed report that Edward Brovarski and I edited with the assistance of Melissa Robinson; she also had the difficult tasks of word processing and organizing the original layout of the manuscript. In the latter job, she was ably assisted by Jennifer Houser who also prepared excellent illustrations. Jordi Ensign and Peter Der Manuelian produced the meticulous preliminary drawings and plans used in the volume, and the latter was also responsible for its design, copy-editing, and production. The staff of the Expedition is indebted to Mrs. Robert P. (Betsey) Nebesar for the invaluable resource she provided in her painstaking transcription of the manuscript of the diary of both the Harvard University-Museum of Fine Arts, Boston excavations at Bersheh in 1915, and of the Reis.

David P. Silverman
General Editor

LIST OF FIGURES

1. The Wadi Deir en-Nakhleh, looking east from the low desert (RG 90/68–31). 4

2. View of the stratum of limestone with quarries and tombs showing the stratum's apparent upward slope (east to west) from the wadi's head to its mouth (RG 90/64–21). 4

3. View of the north side of the wadi showing the high terrace with its nomarchal tombs and the lower tomb terraces (RG 90/85–5). 5

4. View of the south side of the wadi showing the tombs located there (RG 90/85–16). 5

5. View of the open shafts located on the low desert (RG 90/41–4). 6

6. False door from tombs located beneath the modern village of Deir el-Bersheh (DPS 89/10–28). 6

7. View of the high terrace from above (RG 90/81–24). 8

8. Table cross-referencing the various tomb identification systems. 9

9. General view of Tomb 1 looking north (RG 90/65–3). 13

10. Preliminary plan of Tomb 1 (drawing by MR and JRH). 14

11. View of shafts A and B in Tomb 1 (RG 90/65–5). 15

12. Ceiling decoration and texts in Tomb 1 (RG 90/67–23). 16

13. Ceiling decoration in Tomb 5 (RG 90/49–19). 17

14. Traces visible on west wall of Tomb 1 (DPS 90/26–12). 18

15. Traces of decoration and inscription on west wall of Tomb 1 (DPS 90/27–13). 18

16. Traces of decoration and inscription on east wall, north end, of Tomb 1 (drawing by JRH). 19

17. Traces of decoration and inscription on east wall, middle of Tomb 1 (drawing by JRH). 20

18. Traces of decoration and inscription on east wall, south end, of Tomb 1 (DPS 90/19–30). 21

19. Area of ceiling over open shaft (A) in Tomb 1 (DPS 90/26–19). 21

20. Arrangement of texts on the ceiling of Tomb 1 (drawing by BM and JRH). 22

21. Horizontal band of texts in Registers A and B, ceiling of Tomb 1 (RG 90/67–34). 23

22. Ceiling of Tomb 21 with Pyramid Texts and Coffin Texts (drawing by BM and JRH). 24

23. Section of Register C (ceiling of Tomb 1) with a portion of Spell 45, CT I, 193a (drawing by JRH). 25

24. Section of Register C (ceiling of Tomb 1) showing reversed hieroglyphs and bands of stars (RG 90/67–27). 25

25. Layout of registers on the ceiling of Tomb 1 (drawing by MR and JRH). 26

26. Ceiling of Tomb 21 (RG 90/62–33). 27

27. Tomb 7 =EEF 'M' (EG). 28

28. Fallen lintel block from Tomb 18 with titles of the owner, probably the nomarch Amenemhat (drawing by EB and JE). 29

29. Relief from Tomb 18 (drawing by EB and JE). 29

30. Scenes of plowing, harvesting flax, and netting birds from the tomb of Nehri I, Tomb 19 (RG 90/43–31). 31

31. Damaged scene of Nehri I and his wife to the left of the entrance to the inner chamber of Tomb 19 (RG 90/43–23). 32

32. General view of the tomb of Djehutynakht VI, Tomb 21, looking southeast (RG 90/82–9). 33

33. Preliminary plan of Tomb 21 (drawing by MR and JRH). 34

34. View of the collapsed ceiling and shafts in Tomb 21 (RG 90/45–34). 35

35. Preliminary rendering of scene on the right-hand side of the east (rear) wall in Tomb 21 (PDM). 37

36. View of the facades of Tombs 102–104 (right to left; drawing by JRH after *El Bersheh* II, pl. XX). 42

37. Harvard-BMFA Expedition photograph (C 6798; April 25, 1915) showing part of the facade of Tomb 5, the terrace in front of the tomb, and the dump to the far right (courtesy Museum of Fine Arts, Boston). 42

38. Sketch of the Middle Kingdom cemetery (after H. Willems). 43

39. Isometric reconstruction of Tomb 5 showing the walls left after the tomb was quarried in antiquity. 44

40. Attendants from the tomb of Ahanakht (Tomb 5), inner chamber, showing pre-unification canon (courtesy Museum of Fine Arts, Boston). 54

41. Offering bearers from the sarcophagus of Ashait (Cairo, JE 47267) from Deir el-Bahari, reign of Mentuhotep II, pre-reunification (photograph by Bernard V. Bothmer, courtesy Egyptian Museum, Cairo). 54

42. Milking scene from the Tomb of Ahanakht (Tomb 5), inner chamber (drawing by PDM). 54

43. Milking scene from the sarcophagus of Kawit (Cairo JE 47397) from Deir el-Bahari, reign of Mentuhotep II, pre-reunification (courtesy Egyptian Museum, Cairo). 55

44. Milking scene from Giza tomb G 2184, Dynasty V (from W.S. Smith, *History of Egyptian Sculpture and Painting in the Old Kingdom*, fig. 79). 55

45. Jousting bulls from the tomb of Ahanakht (Tomb 5), inner chamber (RG 90/81–11). 55

46. Boatmen assisting cattle across the river, from the tomb of Ahanakht (Tomb 5), outer chamber (RG 90/75–24). 56

47. Large-scale figure of Ahanakht from the east side of the doorway between the chambers in Tomb 5 (RG 90/69–8). 57

48. Large-scale figure of Kaemnofret from his Saqqara tomb chapel, now MFA 04.1761; Dynasty V (RG). 57

49. Geese from south wall of the tomb of Ahanakht (Tomb 5), outer chamber, showing delicate feathering (RG 90/74–2). 58

50. Geese from the coffin of Djehutynakht IV (Tomb 10), showing delicate feathering (MFA 20.1822; courtesy Museum of Fine Arts, Boston). 58

51. Inscription from the tomb of Iha (Tomb 102), showing horizontal and vertical guidelines (RG 90/70–16). 59

52. Inscription from the tomb of Djehutynakht (Tomb 104), showing skewed hieroglyphs (RG 90/79–17) 60

53. Wrestlers from the tomb of Nehri I (Tomb 19; Harvard-BMFA Expedition photograph (C 6837; May 29, 1915; courtesy Museum of Fine Arts, Boston). 62

54. Facade of Tomb D (c) with Fifth Dynasty decree of King Neferefre (RG 90/71–2). 67

55. Effaced figure of Ankhy and accompanying inscriptions from the west wall (DPS 90/27–26). 68

56. View of the west wall with false door and "window" cut through offering scene, Tomb Q (b), the tomb of Ankhy (DPS 90/27–24). 68

57. Doorway to shrine in Tomb S (x), the tomb of Impy (DPS 90/28–16). 69

Initials key

EB	Edward Brovarski
JE	Jordi Ensign
RG	Rus Gant
EG	Edward Gyllenhaal
JRH	Jennifer R. Houser
PDM	Peter Der Manuelian
BM	Brian Muhs
MR	Melissa Robinson
DPS	David P. Silverman

LIST OF ABBREVIATIONS

ÄF	Ägyptologische Forschungen, Glückstadt, Hamburg and New York
ASAE	Annales du Service des Antiquités de l'Egypte, Cairo
ASE	Archaeological Survey of Egypt, London
Bersheh I	E. Newberry, *El Bersheh* I: *The Tomb of Tehutihetep.* London, 1893
Bersheh II	F.Ll. Griffith and P.E. Newberry, *El Bersheh* II. London, 1894
BIFAO	*Bulletin de l'Institut français d'Archéologie orientale,* Cairo
BiOr	*Bibliotheca Orientalis,* Leiden
BMFA	*Bulletin of the Museum of Fine Arts, Boston*
BSEA	British School of Egyptian Archaeology, London
BSFE	*Bulletin de la Societé française d'Egyptologie,* Paris
Chests of Life	Harco Willems, *Chests of Life.* Leiden, 1988
CT	A. de Buck, *The Egyptian Coffin Texts,* vols. 1–7. Chicago, 1935–1961
Eg. Inscriptions	Samuel Sharpe, *Egyptian Inscriptions from the British Museum and other sources.* Moxon, 1855
Egyptian Paintings	Edward L.B. Terrace, *Egyptian Paintings of the Middle Kingdom.* New York and London, 1968
"Ex Oriente Lux"	see *JEOL*
GM	*Göttinger Miszellen,* Göttingen
Grab...ỉnỉ.ỉtỉ.f	B. Jaroš-Deckert, Grabung im Asasif 1963–1970. Band V. *Das Grab des ỉnỉ.ỉtỉ.f. Die Wandmalereien der XI. Dynastie.* Mainz am Rhein, 1984
Hatnub	Rudolf Anthes, *Die Felseninschriften von Hatnub.* Leipzig, 1928
JEOL	*Jaarbericht van het Vooraziatisch-Egyptisch Genootschaap "Ex Oriente Lux,"* Leiden
LÄ	*Lexikon der Ägyptologie,* Wiesbaden
Meir	A.M. Blackman, et al., *The Rock Tombs of Meir,* vols. I–VI. London, 1914–1953
MMJ	*Metropolitan Museum Journal,* New York
Or	*Orientalia,* Nova Series, Rome
RecTrav	*Recueil de Travaux Relatifs à la Philologie et à l'Archéologie Egyptiennes et Assyriennes,* Paris

Studi... Rosellini	*Studi in Memoria di Ippolito Rosellini nel primo centenario della Morte.* Vol. 1, Pisa, 1949
Studies in Anc. Eg.	William K. Simpson and Whitney M. Davis, eds., *Studies in Ancient Egypt, the Aegean, and the Sudan: Essays in Honor of Dows Dunham on the occasion of his 90th birthday, June 1, 1980.* Boston, 1981
Table of Offerings	Edward Brovarski, editor. *A Table of Offerings: 17 Years of Acquisitions of Egyptian and Ancient Near Eastern Art by William Kelly Simpson for the Museum of Fine Arts, Boston.* Boston, 1987
"Textual Criticism"	David P. Silverman, "Textual Criticism in the Coffin Texts," in *Religion and Philosophy in Ancient Egypt.* Edited by William K. Simpson. New Haven, 1989.
UGAÄ	Untersuchungen zur Geschichte und Altertumskunde Ägyptens. Leipzig, Berlin, and Hildesheim
ZÄS	*Zeitschrift fur ägyptische Sprache und Altertumskunde,* Leipzig and Berlin

CHAPTER I

THE BERSHEH NECROPOLIS

Melissa Robinson

A. Physical description of the site

During the First Intermediate Period and Middle Kingdom, Hermopolis, the capital of the Hare (the 15th Upper Egyptian) nome, used a region of low desert and hill-country on the east bank of the Nile as a necropolis. Known as Bersheh today, it is due east of the modern city of Mallawi in the province of Minia. The necropolis is a vast site extending beneath the village of Deir el-Bersheh on the edge of the cultivation, across a strip of low desert (approximately 1 kilometer wide), and up the slope of the Gebel el-Bersheh in the vicinity of the Wadi Deir en-Nakhleh (fig. 1). It was used throughout most of Egyptian history, and remains from the Predynastic Period through the Coptic era have been found.[1]

The region also served as a major site for the quarrying of limestone, mainly during the Late Period, but also in the New Kingdom and perhaps earlier.[2] The hills here were formed of many strata of limestone, and one of the higher layers was of fine quality. Although the wadi's rise in elevation is west to east, this stratum is higher at the wadi's mouth (fig. 2) than at its head. Tombs and quarries are located in this layer on both sides of the wadi.[3] Quarrying efforts on this high terrace ultimately led to the destruction of many of the tombs.[4] The rock overlying this layer was so undermined that it collapsed onto the tombs.[5]

The necropolis of Bersheh, however, is not limited to the high terrace (fig. 3). Other tombs are located at lower elevations in strata of poorer quality limestone on both sides of the mouth of the wadi. On the north side, the path to the high terrace winds its way past them and, on the south side, their counterparts pockmark the hill (fig. 4). In front of the tomb of Ahanakht I on the high terrace, but at a lower elevation, is a group of retainers' tombs. Their existence implies that other nomarchal tombs on the high terrace may also be accompanied by retainer's tombs at this lower elevation.[6] The presence of large talus slopes of quarry and excavation debris elsewhere along this level makes it currently impossible to confirm their presence, although they were reported by earlier excavators.[7]

Mud-brick mastaba tombs, much denuded, also exist in the Bersheh necropolis (fig. 5). The mastaba cemetery extends from the base of the hills north and south of the wadi across the low desert to the cultivation.[8] Excavations by the EAO have confirmed that at least a portion of the mastaba cemetery lies beneath the modern village of Deir el-Bersheh (fig. 6).[9]

At present the Joint Museum of Fine Arts, Boston, Leiden University, University Museum of the University of Pennsylvania Bersheh Expedition is focusing its attention on the tombs of the nomarchs and their subordinates on the high terrace at Bersheh. In the future, we plan to investigate the other cemeteries of the extensive necropolis of Bersheh.

1. Harco Willems, "Deir el-Bersheh: A Preliminary Report," *GM* 110 (1989), pp. 75–95.
2. *El Bersheh* II, pp. 55–56. Fraser discusses the inscriptions found in the wadi dating to the time of Nectanebo II (Nakht-nebef). For the quarry inscriptions of New Kingdom date, see ibid., p. 62 (Thutmosis III) and pp. 63–64 (Amenhotep III); Wilhelm Spiegelberg, "Varia: Die Inschrift Amenophis' III zu el-Bersche," *RecTrav.* 26 (1904), pp. 151–52 and Samuel Sharpe, *Eg. Inscriptions*, pls. 33 and 47 (Thutmosis III). See also R. van Walsem's and Harco Willem's report on p. 41 of this volume.
3. Quarries also exist in a level high on the south side at the wadi's mouth, cf. *El Bersheh* I, pp. 55–57, 63–64, and Willems, *GM* 110 (1989), pp. 75–77.
4. *El Bersheh* II, pp. 56–63. At least one quarry on the high terrace can be dated to the reign of Thutmosis III (ibid., p. 62). Fraser and Blackden, who surveyed the wadi area for the EEF, hypothesized that the tombs themselves were not quarried until the Late Period. They also postulated an earthquake as the ultimate cause of the collapse (ibid., p. 58). See also René van Walsem and Harco Willems, pp. 41–43 in this volume.
5. Willems, *GM* 110 (1989), pp. 75–76.
6. See Willems and van Walsem, pp. 41–43 in this volume.
7. Several shafts or tombs belonging to subordinates of Djehutyhotep were excavated by the expedition led by Georges Daressy in 1897; see Daressy, "Fouilles de Deir el Bircheh (November-Decembre 1897)," *ASAE* 1 (1900), pp. 22–43, especially the map on page 23; see also the map in the publication by Ahmed Bey Kamal, "Fouilles à Deïr-el-Bersheh (mars-avril 1900)," *ASAE* 2 (1901), p. 15. Both maps indicate the presence of subordinates' tombs in front of Djehutyhotep's tomb, but their positions are not readily apparent at the site today, and it is likely that they are buried under the spoil that subsequent excavations added to the talus slope.
8. For excavations on the low desert, see Daressy, "Fouilles," pp. 17–18; Kamal, "Rapport sur les fouilles exécutées à Deir el-Barshé en janvier, février, mars 1901," *ASAE* 2 (1901), pp. 206–7; and Kamal, "Fouilles à Deir-el-Barché exécutées dans les six premiers mois de l'année par M. Antonini de Mallawi," *ASAE* 3 (1902), pp. 281–82. The excavations on the low desert undertaken by George A. Reisner on behalf of the Museum of Fine Arts, Boston remain unpublished. The more recent excavation by the EAO are noted in J. Leclant, "Fouilles et travaux en Egypte et au Soudan, 1969–1970," *Or* 40 (1971), p. 234 and "Fouilles et travaux en Egypte et au Soudan, 1971–1972," *Or* 42 (1973), p. 405.
9. Beneath the village, Mahmud Hamza and Osiris Ghobrial of the EAO uncovered a tomb with a decorated and inscribed burial chamber and false door, belonging to a vizier and nomarch of the Hare nome named Khuu; see ibid., p. 405.

Fig. 1. The Wadi Deir en-Nakhleh, looking east from the low desert.

Fig. 2. View of the stratum of limestone with quarries and tombs (southern side) showing the stratum's apparent upward slope (east-west) from the wadi's head to its mouth.

Fig. 3. View of the north side of the wadi showing the high terrace with its nomarchal tombs and some additional tombs on the lower tomb terraces.

Fig. 4. View of the southern side of the wadi showing the tombs located there.

Fig. 5. View of the open shafts located on the low desert.

Fig. 6. False door from a tomb located beneath the modern village of Deir el-Bersheh.

B. History of work at the site

In 1890–91 P.E. Newberry on behalf of the Egypt Exploration Fund undertook an epigraphic survey of the First Intermediate Period and Middle Kingdom necropolis located on the high terrace (fig. 7).[10] As part of the expedition, G.W. Fraser and M.W. Blackden conducted a walking survey of the Wadi Deir en-Nakhleh and established a base line at the wadi's mouth from which they made their vertical and horizontal measurements. Using these figures, they compiled a sketch map of the area. In total they identified thirty-six rock-cut tombs on the northern side and seventy-two rock-cut tombs (and numerous shafts) on the southern side.[11]

They assigned alphanumeric designations to each of the tombs they located. The decorated tombs on the high terrace were identified by number and mapped individually.[12] Their approximate locations were then noted on a sketch map of the terrace as well as the area sketch map. Fraser and Blackden gave all other archaeological features (quarries, tombs and tomb groups, on both north and south sides of the wadi) alphabetic identifications: uppercase for quarries and important tombs and groups, lowercase for individual tombs within a group. Finally, using the information they had gathered, Newberry noted the approximate positions of the quarries, tombs, and tomb groups by letter on the area sketch map.[13]

In 1897 and from 1900–1902 expeditions under the auspices of the Egyptian Antiquities Service and led by Georges Daressy and Ahmed Kamal respectively undertook the archaeological exploration of the Bersheh necropolis.[14] Each individual conducted work both on the low desert and on the north side of the wadi. Considered together, their excavations on the low desert uncovered over forty tombs of Middle Kingdom date with mud-brick shafts and one or two burial chambers. Although the tombs had been looted in antiquity, the excavations recovered pottery, stone vessels, coffin fragments, and various small finds.[15]

Daressy and Kamal also focused their attention on the tombs in the vicinity of the high terrace, most specifically Tombs 18 and 19, and those belonging to Djehutyhotep's subordinates (near Tomb 20).[16] While most of the tombs had been opened in antiquity, the excavators recovered a wealth of material from the burial chambers: model boats, granaries and servants, model food and tools, pottery, stone vessels, and most importantly for our study of Egyptian religion, coffins inscribed with Coffin Texts. Daressy also investigated several very deep shafts on the summit which contained funerary objects and coffins.[17]

Artists from each of these expeditions produced a sketch map showing the location of the shafts in which they worked. Daressy instituted his own alphabetically based tomb identification system (upper and lower case). Kamal, on the other hand, built upon the numerical system begun by the EEF expedition for the high terrace and renumbered the shafts opened by Daressy. Unfortunately the tombs on the low desert were not included in either system.

In 1915, George A. Reisner, sponsored by the Harvard University-Museum of Fine Arts, Boston Expedition, directed the most extensive excavations at the site, both on the high terrace and on the low desert, but the results of this work remain almost totally unpublished.[18] The Harvard-Boston Expedition, too, developed another system for the identification of the tombs. Those located on the high terrace received numbers from 1–99, those lower on the slope, i.e., the retainers' tombs, numbers from 100–199, and those on the low desert, numbers from 1000–2999. The expedition also produced a map of the high terrace, which unfortunately does not include either EEF Tombs 1, 8, 9, and 10 or many of the shafts discovered by Daressy and Kamal.

10. *El Bersheh* I and *El Bersheh* II. For an overview of archaeological work at the site, see T. Zimmer, "La Moyenne Egypte: methodes d'investigation bibliographiques et priorités," *BSFE* 96 (1983), pp. 22–25.

11. *El Bersheh* II, pp. 56 and 65.

12. The numbers run from west to east (1–7) on the high terrace, but the retainers' tombs are numbered from east to west (8–10); see ibid., pp. 58–63 and plate III.

13. Ibid., plates II (area sketch map signed by Newberry) and III (terrace map).

14. Daressy, "Fouilles...," pp. 17–43, especially the map on p. 23; Kamal, "Fouilles... (Mars-Avril 1900)," pp. 14–23, especially the map on p. 15; Kamal, "Rapport," pp. 206–21; and Kamal, "Fouilles... M. Antonini de Mallawi," pp. 276–81.

15. Daressy, "Fouilles...," pp. 17–18, Kamal, "Rapport," pp. 206–7, Kamal, "Fouilles... M. Antonini de Mallawi," pp. 276–7, 281–82.

16. Daressy. "Fouilles...," pp. 23–42, Kamal, "Fouilles... (Mars-Avril 1900)," and "Rapport," pp. 14–43 and pp. 208–21, and Kamal,"Fouilles... M. Antonini de Mallawi," pp. 277–81.

17. Daressy, "Fouilles...,"*ASAE* 1, pp. 18–22.

Fig. 7. View, looking west, of the high terrace on the northern side of the wadi from the top of Tomb 5.

In conclusion, although the Bersheh necropolis has received considerable attention, it remains at best only partially mapped, and the different tomb identification systems devised by the various expeditions have been extremely confusing to researchers during the intervening decades. For the time being, the Joint Bersheh Expedition has decided to follow the numbering system that Reisner developed. The table in fig. 8 provides cross-references for the various tomb identification systems.

18. For a brief overview of this expedition, see: Edward L. B. Terrace, *Egyptian Paintings*, pp. 20–24. For a brief report on the discoveries found in Reisner Tomb 10, see Dows Dunham, "The Tomb of Dehuti-nekht and His Wife, about 2000 B.C.," *BMFA* 19 (1921), pp. 43–46. Several field photos of Tomb 5 have been published by Edward Brovarski, "Ahanakht of Bersheh and the Hare Nome in the First Intermediate Period and Middle Kingdom," in *Studies in Anc. Eg.*, pp. 14–30. Some objects from the Harvard-MFA, Boston excavations have been published in *Mummies and Magic: The Funerary Arts of Ancient Egypt*, edited by Sue D'Auria, Peter Lacovara, and Catharine H. Roehrig, (Boston: Museum of Fine Arts, 1988), pp. 109–17 (Tomb 10), 120 (Tomb 20), and 124–25 (Tombs 13 and 19). For the coffin of Djehutynakht, see, Terrace, *Egyptian Paintings*, pp. 32–41 and pls. I–XLIV and Dows Dunham and William Stevenson Smith, "A Middle Kingdom painted Coffin from Deir el Bersheh," in *Studi... Rosellini*, vol. 1, pp. 261–68 and pls. xxi–xxvii. See also Edward Brovarski, *Canopics*, pp. 85–86 and 89–91 (Tomb 10), 92–93 (Tomb 13), 94–95 (Tomb 51), and 87–88 (Tomb 2001).

REISNER	EEF	DARESSY	KAMAL	TOMB OWNER OR OTHER NAME
1	7			Nehri II
2				
3				
4	6		6	Djehutynakht VII
5	5		5	Ahanakht I
6				
7	M(?)			[...]-dua
8				
9				
10				Djehutynakht IV or V
11				Bik
12				
13				
(18)	3		3 (21, 22, 23)	Amenemhat and Sep
19	4		4 (26)	Nehri I
20	2		2 (24, 25, 27)	Djehutyhotep and Kay
21	1		1	Djehutynakht VI
51				
102	8		8	Iha
103	9		9	Khnumnakht
104	10		10	Djehutynakht
	K			
	L			
	N			Ahanakht II (cf. *GM* 110)
		No label	11	Sen(?)
		G	12	Gua
		F	13	Nefri
		E	14	Sepi II and Sepi III
		D	15	Sepi I
		A(?)	16	Unfinished
		C	17	Satipi and Ankhu
		B	18	Nebirut
	G(?)	a	19	
	G(?)	b	20	Sat-hedjet-hetep
	D (c)			Decree of Neferefre
	Q (b)			Ankhy
	S (x)			Impy

Fig. 8. Table cross-referencing the various tomb identification systems. Question marks within parentheses indicate that the cross-reference between different tomb identification systems is not absolutely positive. The number 18 was unused by the Reisner expedition but has been assigned to EEF 3 by the current project. Numbers within parentheses are the numerical identifications given by Kamal to shafts that he excavated on the high terrace on the northern side of the wadi. Capital letters with small letters within parentheses are the alphabetic identifications that Fraser gave tombs not located on the high terrace.

CHAPTER II

TOMBS ON THE HIGH TERRACE

Melissa Robinson

David P. Silverman

Edward Brovarski

A. Reisner 1 – The Tomb of Nehri II

1. Physical Description

This tomb (fig. 9) is rectangular in shape, 6.0 meters square +/–0.05 meters, with the rear wall at local north (the left rear corner corresponds roughly to magnetic north). It has suffered from extensive quarrying. The left and rear walls are preserved from floor to ceiling, but the entire remaining front wall and the front 4.0 meters of the right are now less than 1.0 meter high (fig. 10). The rear 2.0 meters of the left wall contains a poorly preserved false door. The ceiling is approximately 2.3 meters high (measured from the current floor level at the walls). In the center of the rear wall is a shaft, C, with roughly hewn walls and floor; the latter, roughly 5.0 meters long, slopes down at approximately 20 degrees.

Cut in the floor of the chamber are two more shafts A (east) and B (west), both apparently cleared by Kamal (fig. 11).[19] Shaft A is now open to a depth of about 7.0 meters, but no burial chamber is visible. It is rectangular in shape, measuring roughly 1.90 x 3.85 meters, and it is located 1.25 meters from the north wall of the tomb and 1.06 meters from the east wall.[20] Its southeastern corner is occupied by an overhang of compacted shaft fill. Carved in the stone near two corners of the shaft are the hand and footholds used by the ancient workmen to gain access to the shaft during its construction and then for the subsequent burial. B is also rectangular in plan, but unlike A it is now filled to

19. *Bersheh Diary* (Harvard University-Museum of Fine Arts, Boston Bersheh Expedition 1915), p. 5.

20. This shaft was actually cut in two stages. First an area measuring 2.21 x 4.0 meters was cut into the floor to a depth of about 0.15 meters. Then the shaft itself was cut within this area. The result is a rabbeted opening with a ledge +/– 0.10 meters wide along the west, north and east sides that forms a recess into which slabs of stone would have been set to close the entrance to the shaft.

Fig. 9. General view of Tomb 1, the tomb of Nehri II, looking towards local north. Note the extent to which the east and south walls of the tomb have been quarried.

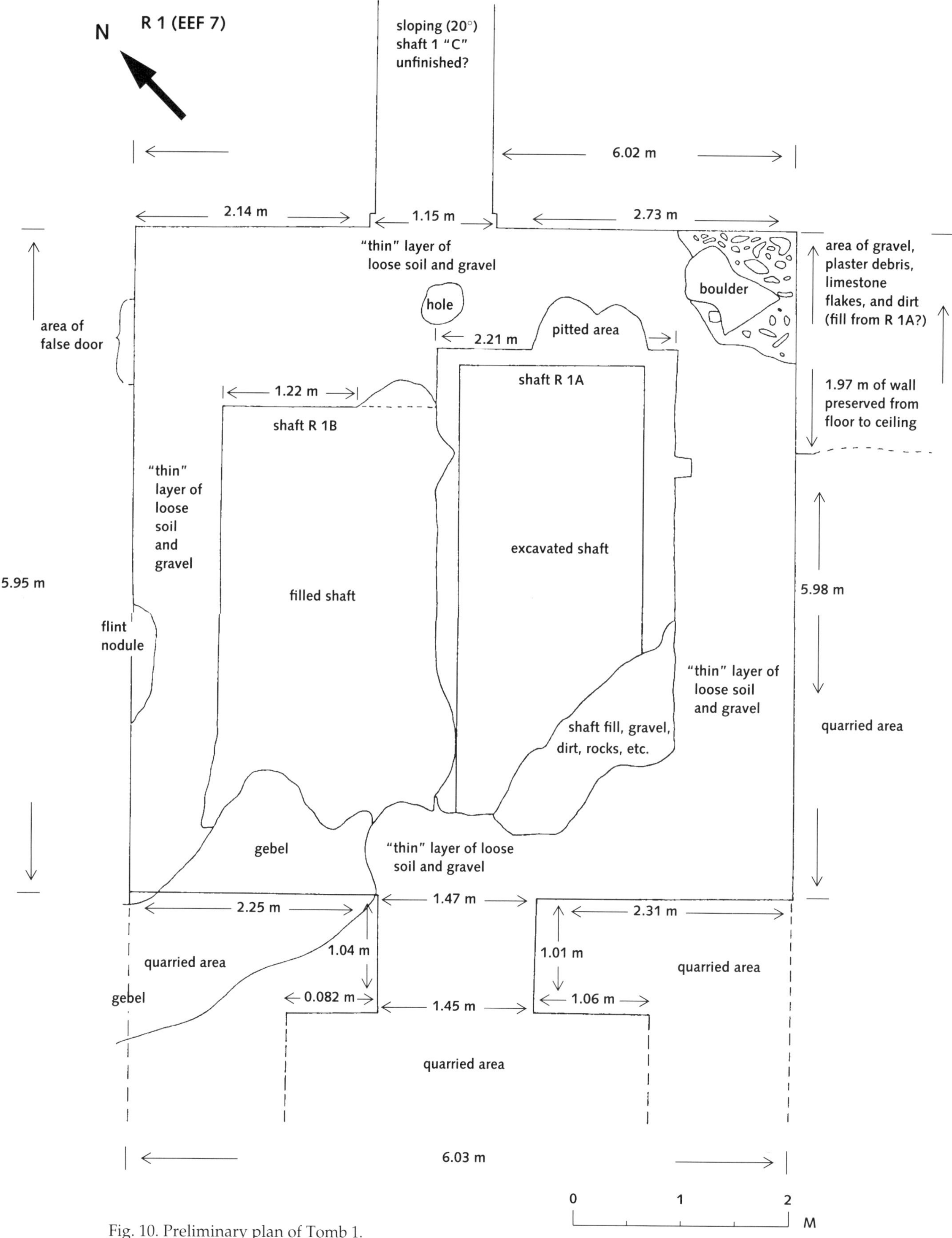

Fig. 10. Preliminary plan of Tomb 1.

Fig. 11. Shafts A, B and C in Tomb 1. The overhang of compacted fill that made work in this tomb hazardous is located in the lower right corner of the right shaft (A). Note also the hand- and footholds in the rear wall of shaft A and the rabbeting around shaft C.

within 0.10 meters of the floor's surface, and no interior details are visible. It measures about 1.90 x 3.75 meters and is located 1.59 meters from the north wall of the tomb and 0.82 meters from the west wall.

Access to the tomb was originally gained via a small outer forecourt or chamber on the south which has been mostly quarried away. The north wall of this area measured approximately 3.33 meters in length and is preserved to a maximum height of under 0.50 meters. The entrance passage to the tomb itself is 1.45–1.47 meters wide, and its western and eastern walls measure 1.04 and 1.01 meters in length respectively.

2. *Epigraphic Work in the Tomb of Nehri II*

The team of epigraphers from the University Museum began the season recording inscriptions in Tomb 1. It belonged to the nomarch Nehri II who lived during the reign of Sesostris I.[21] The relatively stable condition of the decorated ceiling, the large number of texts, and its favorable location in regard to a natural light source made it an ideal project. The authors of the original publication had considered the ceiling with its well-preserved religious text to be the most notable feature of the tomb,[22] and they had recorded what was visible to them at the time. Unfortunately, the copy they published was not completely accurate,[23] and, therefore, the directors of the present expedition decided that it was necessary to produce a new copy of the texts.

The ceiling still retains much of its original decoration which had been carved in a smooth coating of plaster that covered the entire surface and then painted. The overall plan has several horizontal registers of texts within which are hieroglyphs arranged mainly in vertical columns. The signs are painted blue, and the background is a cream color. Alternating with the textual registers are horizontal bands containing only large five-pointed stars (fig. 12). Like the hieroglyphs, they are blue; the background, however, is a darker yellow-cream color. This latter color scheme represents a reversal of the

21. See Harco Willems, *Chests of Life*, p. 71; he refers (p. 20) to the tomb as source B1B. For discussion of the genealogy, see also Brovarski, "Ahanakht of Bersheh," *Studies in Anc. Eg.*, p. 22; and Willems, "Nomarchs of the Hare Nome," *JEOL* 28 (1983–84), pp. 80–102.

22. *El Bersheh* II, p. 37.

23. Ibid., pl. XIX, and see below, pp. 17, 20.

Fig. 12. Ceiling decoration and texts in Tomb 1.

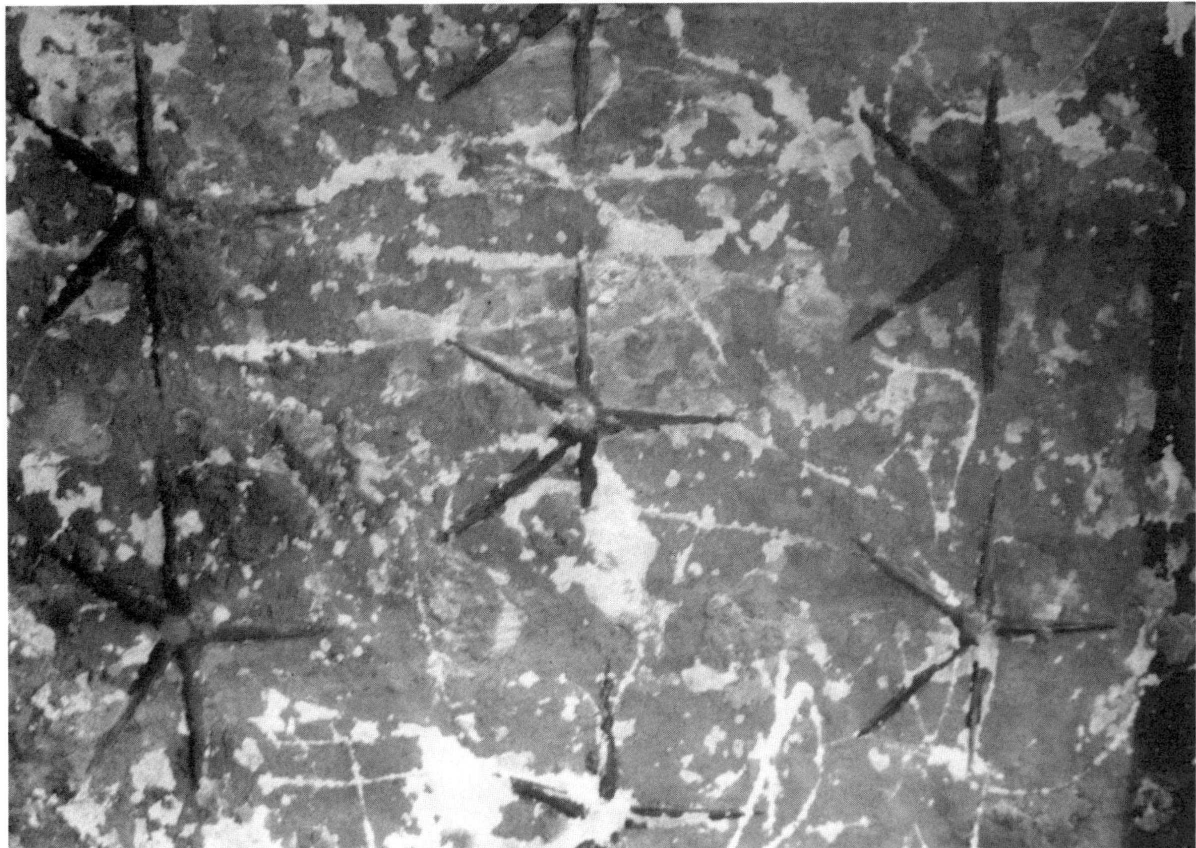

Fig. 13. Ceiling decoration in Tomb 5.

traditional arrangement of a lighter figure on a darker background; this variation, however, occurs elsewhere at Bersheh (fig. 13).[24]

Griffith and Newberry recorded only the inscriptions on the ceiling, and they noted that the texts[25] were not identical with but similar to those of the Book of the Dead. In regard to the tomb itself, they commented that "it was entirely destroyed." They remarked further that "there are a few traces of painted *kheker* ornament at the top of the walls, but all vestiges of the paintings below have been destroyed."[26]

The identification of the texts on the ceiling, as noted above, was not quite correct, but a preliminary examination of the walls seemed at first to corroborate the authors' description. Closer inspection by the staff, however, revealed traces of paint and indications of carved hieroglyphs (fig. 14). The preservation of the wall surface was poor, since much of the plaster coating had fallen off taking most of the decoration with it. Moreover, numerous modern and ancient graffiti defaced a large part of what still remained on the wall.

Careful brushing and preliminary cleaning under the guidance of the conservator, however, revealed sufficient traces of color and some carved lines to suggest a good deal of the original decorative scheme on the left (west) and right (east) walls. The epigraphers were able to trace on clear acetate the remnants of paint and carving on the bits of plaster that still adhered to the wall and the faint lines that the ancient chisels had left below the plaster covering. In copying the figures and the hieroglyphic signs the epigraphers used fine-tipped pens and coordinated the inks to correspond with the ancient colors. Thus, they were able to recover much of the original scene and the text (fig. 15).

A fairly long horizontal inscription, reading from left to right (south to north), went across much of the mid-section of the left (west) wall: *ḥtp dỉ nswt*

24. This reversed color scheme occurs in the tomb of Ahanakht I (*El Bersheh* II, p. 31, fig. 13); the more usual arrangement occurs, however, in Tomb 21, the tomb of Djehutynakht VI.

25. Ibid., p. 37.

26. Ibid.

Fig. 14. Traces of inscription visible on the west wall of Tomb 1.

Fig. 15. Traces of decoration and inscription on the west wall of Tomb 1 as recorded on acetate (in situ).

ḥtp dỉ ỉnpw, followed by a destroyed area in which epithets of the god undoubtedly occurred. A funerary request follows: *[...]⸗f ḥr wꜣwt nfrt [nbt] n(t) ẖrt-nṯr*, "May he [travel] upon [all] the beautiful roads of the necropolis."[27] Beyond were designations of the tomb owner that the epigraphers found elsewhere in the tomb: *ỉmꜣḫy ḥꜣty-ꜥ ẖrp nsty ỉmy-r ḥmw-nṯr Nḥrỉ*, "the revered one, hereditary prince, controller of the two thrones, overseer of prophets, Nehri." The phrase *ms.n N[...]*, occurred after the name of the deceased, and it indicates that Nehri II was born to a woman whose name began with the letter *N*. Until this discovery, there had been no knowledge of the tomb owner's parentage.[28] The entire inscription runs approximately one half the length of the left (west) wall.

A second register below the first contains an offering list inscribed in small blue hieroglyphs similar to that found in the tombs of Ahanakht (Tomb 5) nearby and Djehutynakht (Tomb 21).[29] A third register, below the menu, preserves traces of the figures of several kneeling offering bearers, similar to those found in the tombs just mentioned. The uppermost register with the funerary prayer continues across the wall up to two large scale figures, while the two lower registers end at mid-wall; the remaining space is then occupied by a pile of offerings surmounted by a *bꜣk* (moringa) plant, a motif found in other tombs on the high terrace at Bersheh.[30] Other recognizable items are figs and a haunch of beef (see fig. 15). Bits of blue paint and faint chisel lines reveal what appears to be two figures who face outward (south), undoubtedly Nehri and perhaps his wife or mother. Possible traces of a smaller figure, perhaps a child, occur in front of Nehri. A deeply carved false door behind the couple shows no remaining surface decoration, but a close examination of the area between it and the back wall revealed a few hieroglyphic signs, suggesting the presence of another inscription.

As of yet, we have found no remnant of the decoration on the back wall except for fragments of paint from a *kheker* frieze at the top of the wall (Presumably such a frieze was originally on all the walls of the chamber). There is a rectangular opening in the middle of the wall, and its edge is recessed, presumably to fit a slab that would cover the sloping shaft beyond.

Only a small portion of the right (east) wall still remains standing; its surface is extremely rough, and today it retains virtually none of its original plaster or paint. Still, traces of the original scene and some text could be made out (fig. 16). Two figures stand toward the back of the wall; the larger, presumably Nehri, holds a staff, while the other figure, perhaps his wife or mother, is behind him.

Fig. 16. Traces of standing figures, facing right, and inscriptions on the east wall, north end, of Tomb 1.

27. Winfried Barta, *Aufbau und Bedeutung der altägyptischen Opferformel*, ÄF 24 (Glückstadt-Hamburg: J.J. Augustin, 1968), pp. 60, Bitte 12.

28. Although the section is heavily damaged, the signs are clear. It is unlikely that the second *n* is due to dittography. *Nḥrỉ ms.n* is just visible at the top of fig. 15.

29. *El Bersheh* II, frontispiece.

30. See the discussion of this motif by R. Freed, pp. 62 n. 139, in this volume.

Fig. 17. Traces of swamp scene and accompanying inscription on the east wall, middle, of Tomb 1.

The two face outward (south), and at least three registers of smaller figures are discernible in the area before them. Several hieroglyphs could also be made out near the figures. Only the lowest part of the central and southern section of the wall still stands, and after preliminary cleaning, a small part of the original scene became visible: a bird, papyrus clumps, and some text (fig. 17). Such imagery suggests a swamp scene, a motif that can also be found in a bottom register in the tomb of Ahanakht (Tomb 5).[31] The lower section of the southernmost part of the right (east) wall also showed traces of another inscription (fig. 18). The southern or entrance wall is almost totally destroyed, and thus far, no trace of the decoration has been discovered. Future cleaning may reveal even more of the decoration of Tomb 1.

In contrast to the rest of the tomb, the ceiling and the texts on it are still in good condition. Although not complete today, the portion that is intact retains most of its original plaster coating with carved and painted hieroglyphs. Nevertheless, the fragility of the yellow and blue pigments and the underlying plaster necessitated the use of hand copies and photography rather than direct tracing as the preferred method for recording the texts. All of the texts were photographed on a uniform scale. The resulting prints will be seamed together and then traced. This copy will be collated with the hand copies and then collated against the inscriptions next season. While the photographing process was being completed, the epigraphers made several hand copies and collations of the text. Re-copying these texts for publication was necessary, for Newberry's version contained some errors, had some incorrect orientations of hieroglyphs, and omitted some texts.

Many of the texts that Newberry had neglected to include occur on the part of the ceiling that is situated over a section of the floor in which an open burial shaft is now located (fig. 19). Whether Newberry's team had difficulty dealing with the same obstacle (see fig. 11), is not clear, for although Fraser in his description notes the probability of two or three great shafts in the floor,[32] the expedition evidently did not completely clear either shaft, and the artist did not include an indication of the shafts on the plan.[33] The present staff built a temporary wooden cover over the shaft to serve as a platform upon which the epigraphers could stand safely and record accurately all of the texts on the ceiling.

The inscriptions on the ceiling are drawn from the collection mainly of Coffin Texts, a fact which was clear even from Newberry's copies. The texts are to be read from left to right (west to east), and the spells thus far identified are as follows: Register A–1029; B–1071/1181, 1072/1182, 1073/1183, and 1079; C–44a, 45b, 44b, 45a; D–384, 216, 385, 389, 421, 423; E–353, 413, 215, 388, 109, 361; F–205, 434, 488, 491, PT 677 (fig. 20).[34] A fragmentary register (G) at the very back of the ceiling had a single row of larger hieroglyphs whose now fragmentary text appears to consist of the titles, epithets, and name of the deceased.

Most of the spells on the ceiling occur elsewhere at Bersheh and some at other sites as well. Those in Registers A and B are, however, specifically associated with this particular site. Interestingly the texts in Register B are treated

31. *El Bersheh* II, pl. XV.

32. *El Bersheh* II, p. 62.

33. Ibid., pl. XVIII.

34. The schematic plan was drawn by Brian Muhs and Peter Der Manuelian.

Fig. 18. Traces of decoration and inscription on the east wall, south end, of Tomb 1.

Fig. 19. Area of the ceiling over open shaft (A) in Tomb 1.

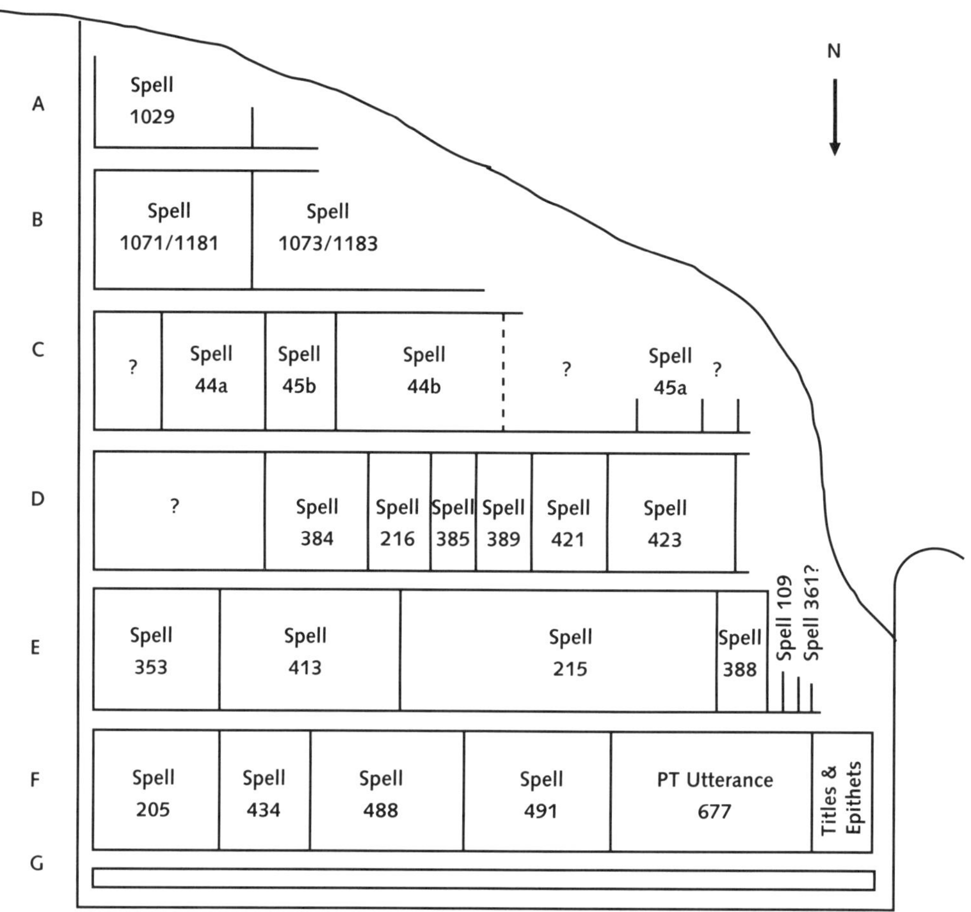

Fig. 20. Schematic plan of the ceiling of Tomb 1 showing the arrangement of texts.

distinctly from the others on the ceiling. Here, the inscriptions are oriented horizontally, as well as vertically, whereas those in Register C–F are always in columns. (There is very little left of Register A, but the preserved texts appear in vertical columns) Neither the size nor the orientation of the signs in Register B are as consistent as they are in the other registers. In some of the spells, the hieroglyphs at the bottom of the register intrude into the space of the horizontal bands between the registers of texts (fig. 21). One whole passage is even written upside down. While this lack of organization may seem unusual, similar patterns occur on the floor boards of several coffins. In fact, those spells recorded in Register B are precisely those that appear with alternating orientation in the coffins.[35] The overall design of the ceiling, bands of texts alternating with registers, either blank or decorated, is another feature that relates the ceiling to coffins, for that arrangement is paralleled on coffin lids.

The funerary nature of the texts on the ceiling is not unique to the tomb of Nehri II; both Pyramid and Coffin Texts were also inscribed on the ceiling of Reisner Tomb 21 (fig. 22) as well as on a loose block, perhaps also from the same tomb. Further investigation of the tombs on this terrace may provide more information about the extent of the use of funerary texts as decoration in the tombs at Bersheh.

During the process of identifying which of the Coffin Texts had appeared on the ceiling of Nehri II's tomb, a comparison between the new versions with those published by de Buck was made. The texts from Nehri II closely followed the

35. See the organization of texts for the Spells 101, 1072, 1073 and 1079 in Adriaan de Buck, *The Egyptian Coffin Texts* VII, pp. 334–351.

Fig. 21. Horizontal band of texts in Registers A and B on the ceiling of Tomb 1.

other versions, but Nehri's scribe(s) occasionally deviated from the version found in other sources. For example, Spell 45 which appears in Register C should contain the word *ḫ3t* "offering table" (CT I, 193 a). Nehri's scribe replaced it with the similar sounding, but distinct word *ḥ3t* "corpse," a writing not attested elsewhere (fig. 23). Such a variation does not appear to represent conscious editing, because the context requires the expression "the offering tables of Re" rather than, "the corpses of Re."[36]

This error in the Nehri version appears rather to have been the result of a hearing error; the scribe taking dictation simply wrote down what he heard.[37] If such was the case, then it is likely that the draughtsman did not transcribe the text from a hieratic copy on papyrus, but rather inscribed the signs as they were read aloud from such a papyrus by another individual. It is alternately possible that the "hearing error" was introduced into the master copy earlier and that the copyists working in Nehri's tomb used a faulty manuscript. While there is no direct evidence against this latter suggestion, it seems less likely, since no other version of the spell has a similar orthography for this word. Applying the signs directly from dictation, moreover, would also account for the carelessness in the execution of

36. Silverman, "Textual Criticism," pp. 32–34.

37. While *ḫ3yt* (*Wb.* III, p. 224, 13–14) and *ḫ3(w)t* (*Wb.* II, p. 226, 11–19) "offering table" show no variants with *ḥ*, a perhaps similar sounding word *ḫ3yt* (*Wb.* III, p. 224, 6–11) "sickness" seems to have a variant spelling *ḥ3t* (*Wb.* III, p. 360, 5). The scribe may well have confused all of these words. For other hearing errors, see G. Fecht, *Wortakzent und Silbenstruktur,* ÄF 21 (Glückstadt: J.J. Augustin, 1960), notes 199, 241, 275, 400 and § 206. (I am grateful to Dr. J. Allen for directing me to this reference). See also, Silverman, "Textual Criticism," p. 60, and the remarks of B. Van de Walle, *La transmission des textes littéraires égyptiennes,* pp. 10–11.

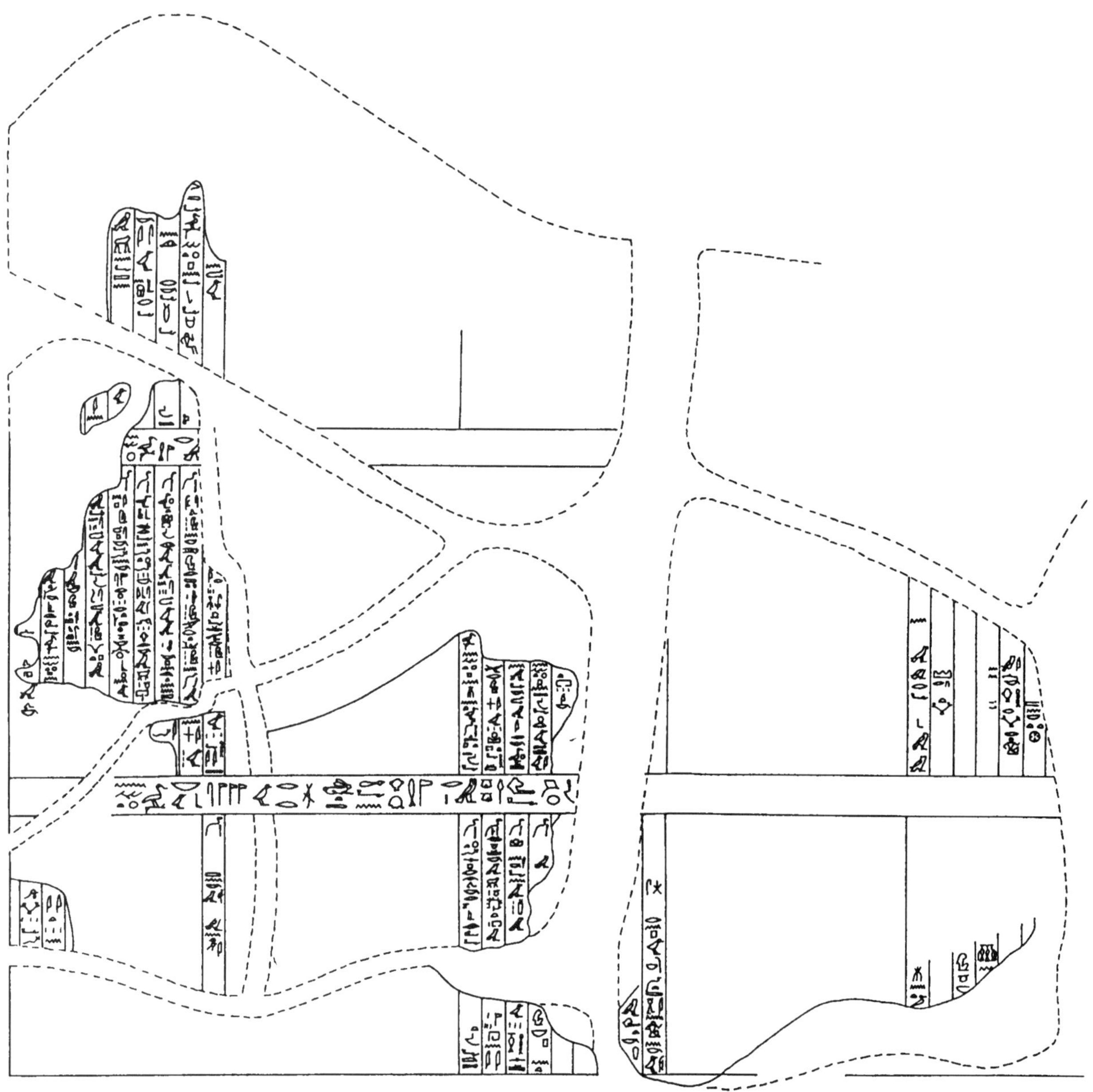

Fig. 22. Schematic plan of the Pyramid and Coffin Texts on the ceiling of Tomb 21.

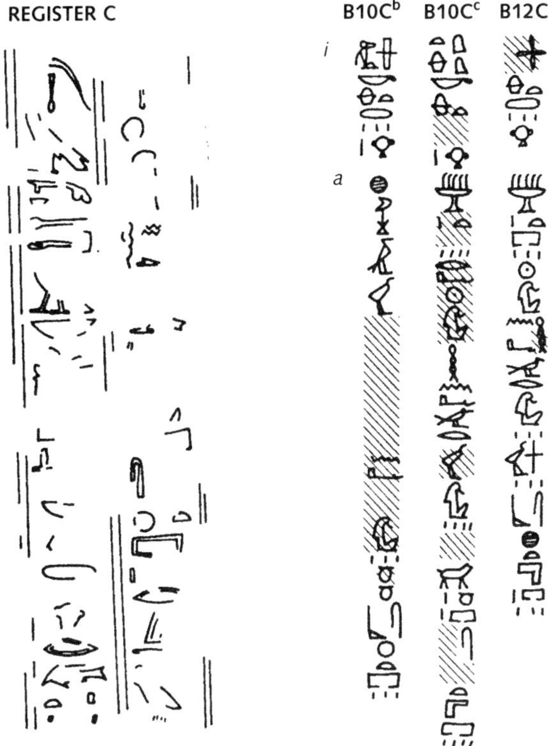

Fig. 23. Section of Register C (ceiling of Tomb 1) with a portion of Spell 45, CT I 193a.

Fig. 24. Section of Register C (ceiling of Tomb 1) showing reversed hieroglyphs and the bands of stars.

some signs, and the reversal of almost all 𓅓 (*mꜣꜣ*) and 𓋴 (*s*) hieroglyphs (fig. 24).

It was awkward to transcribe a text on a ceiling in the best of circumstances. Having to refer constantly to a written text would have made the task even more difficult. The most likely procedure then would have been for the artisan/scribe to work from a plan of the ceiling inscribed on papyrus for the arrangement of the registers, texts, and decorative patterns, but to rely on dictation for the recording of the texts. Based on the observations just noted above, it is quite apparent that the overseer of the tomb project was not careful in checking the texts on the ceiling against the original manuscript. Another peculiarity of the texts which may also be due to the dictation is that a generalized bird is often written for the hieroglyph for *wr* (𓅨 swallow) and for *ꜣ* (𓄿 vulture).

Those who were responsible for the construction of the tomb, however, took considerable care when they carved it out of the rock, judging from the precise measurements of the almost square floor plan and the fairly consistent height of all the walls. The precision did not extend to decoration on the ceiling, and close examination reveals some inconsistencies. For example, while the scribe followed the usual tradition of not indicating in any specific manner the end of a spell, occasionally he did indicate a break by leaving a blank space or even a whole blank column, before beginning a new spell.

The epigraphers who copied the texts this season had the distinct impression that the upper and lower lines that bordered the registers sloped downward and converged as one looked across the ceiling from left to right (west-east). These lines did not appear to remain at a consistent distance from each other. Careful measuring of the height of the registers confirmed these observations: the distance between the top and bottom of some registers did indeed increase from left to right. In fact, some registers showed a discrepancy of more than 15 centimeters when comparing the height on the left to that on the right (fig. 25). To compensate for the progressively lower height, the scribes were forced to diminish the size of the hieroglyphs. The decorative bands between the registers fluctuated in height correspondingly.

Strangely, however, the five-pointed stars within the bands appeared to remain constant in

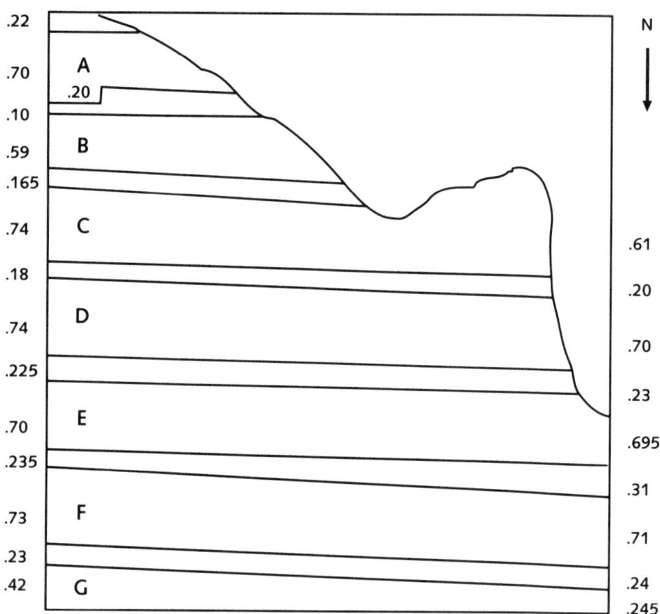

Fig. 25. Schematic plan showing the layout of registers and bands on the ceiling of Tomb 1.

size. They did not seem to get smaller, and in some cases they overlapped the lower border of the register and intruded into the area of texts. It was necessary, therefore, to measure as many of the preserved stars as possible, and, in so doing, it was discovered that each star was approximately 20 cm. high. The stars to the left fit within their borders, but those to the right, did not remain within their confines (See fig. 24). Careful examination of all of the stars also revealed that each had a distinctly shorter lower left leg and that the distance from the bottom of that leg to the top of the uppermost point was consistently about 18 cms. The overall uniformity of the size and shape of the stars, the apparent lack of any attempt to alter their size so that they would fit wholly within their registers, and their distinctive shorter leg are all factors that would suggest that the stars were not drawn freehand, but were produced through the use of a template.[38] Tracing from a template or pattern for the stars, but not the hieroglyphs, would explain why the artist could adjust the signs to fit the space available, but not the stars, and it also would account for the consistency in size and shape of the stars in this tomb.

[38] Petrie pointed out the use of brands or color stamps that dated from the 18th Dynasty; see *Tools and Weapons*, pp. 56–7 (I am indebted to Charles Van Siclen for bringing this parallel to my attention). See also the section by R. van Walsem, pp. 47–48 in this volume for other discoveries about techniques of decoration at Bersheh.

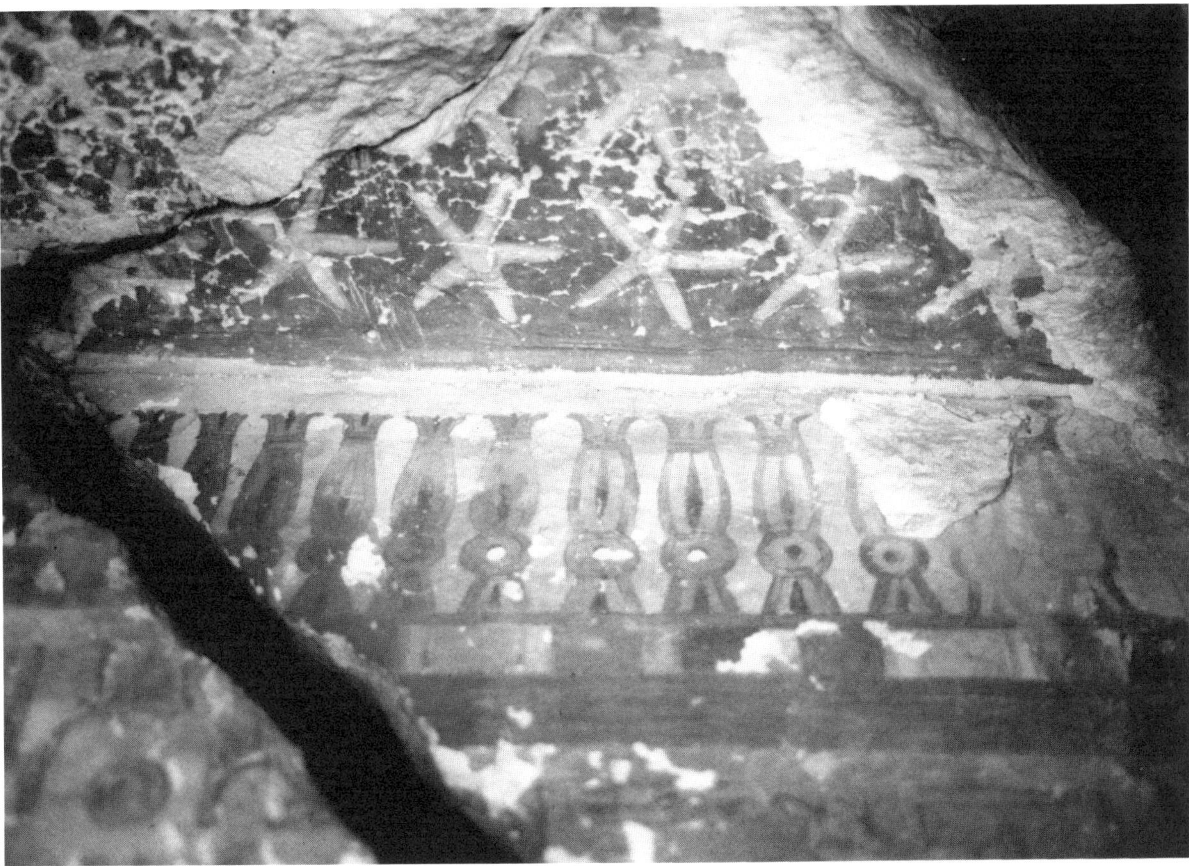

Fig. 26. Stars on a section of the damaged ceiling of the shrine in Tomb 21.

Examination of the ceiling patterns in other tombs at Bersheh revealed other probable examples of the use of templates. The Tomb of Ahanakht (No. 5), has on its ceiling a simple star pattern, and although the paint obscures the edges, the carved form reveals consistency in the size and shape of each star (see fig. 13). The ceiling of the shrine in tomb no. 21 has a star pattern similar to that of Nehri, and there too, a lower left leg is shorter (fig. 26). If this suggestion about the use of templates for the stars in the ceiling decoration in this tomb is accepted, then it can perhaps be extended to other types of repetitive motifs, such as *kheker* friezes. Examinations of such a hypothesis, along with additional epigraphy, awaits the second season of epigraphic work at Bersheh.

B. Tomb 7 (=EEF 'M')

In front of the nomarch's tombs on the high terrace was a series of smaller tombs, oblong in plan, with entrances on the south and a single shaft in the center.[39] All the walls were quarried to within a few inches of the floor (fig. 27), and Tomb 7 (see fig. 27) is the only one of these tombs to preserve any vestiges of decoration.[40] A deeply cut false door on the west wall preserves the terminal letters of the owner's name: a vulture and a kneeling man with arms outstretched in prayer, probably to be read *dwꜣ*. To the left of the false door is a damaged register executed in low sunk relief. On the right is a milking scene with a diminutive figure of a dairyman kneeling at a cow's udder. The scene closely resembles another in the tomb of the nomarch Ahanakht.[41] Although badly damaged, the scene on the left may show two hunting dogs attacking a wild bull.

C. Tomb 18 – The Tomb of Amenemhat

Work was also initiated this season in Tomb 18,

39. See the map in Terrace, *Egyptian Paintings*, p. 12.

40. Cf. Fraser, in *El Bersheh* II, p. 61.

41. Ibid., plate XIV; see below, p. 53.

Fig. 27. Tomb 7 (=EEF 'M').

which had been nearly completely destroyed by quarrying. The fallen lintel block that Newberry published[42] clearly formed part of an impressive entrance to the tomb with hieroglyphs over 18 cm. tall (fig. 28). Two other fragments, both from the west or left end of the lintel still remain; one is in situ and the other nearly so. In addition, the top of the outermost column of the left-hand jamb still stands. It is clear that four incised lines of text, reading from right to left, originally occupied the lintel and continued on the jambs in an unknown number of columns.

Newberry and Griffith assigned the tomb to the "Royal Scribe" Sep because of a damaged false door belonging to *Sp ỉr.n Wȝḏ-kȝw≠s*. From the evidence of another relief, it appears that Sep was probably a son of the nomarch Amenemhat and Wadjkaues (fig. 29).[43] In point of fact, the false door occupied a niche or "shrine" in the northeast corner of its courtyard. Since Ahmed Kamal found the coffins of the nomarch Amenemhat (CG 28091/92) in a great pit in its interior, it is more likely that Reisner 18 belonged to the latter. Amenemhat was a son of Nehri II and probably succeeded his brother as nomarch at the end of the reign of Sesostris I or in the early reign of Amenemhat II.[44] This season part of the name of Amenemhat's mother *[Sȝt-ḥ]ḏt-ḥtp* was found at the end of two lines on the left-side of the section of the lintel still in situ, and it is possible that traces of the *mn*-sign and *m* of the nomarch's name remain on the misplaced block just to the right.

D. Tomb 19 – The Tomb of Nehri I

Several days were spent copying the accessible reliefs in Tomb 19 which belonged to Nehri I, a prominent figure in the historically significant Hatnub graffiti.[45] The tomb consists of two chambers, both

42. Ibid., II, p. 27.

43. Ibid., pp. 27–28. The latter relief is now in Boston (MFA 1972.984); see Edward Brovarski, ed., *A Table of Offerings*, pp. 10–11.

44. Brovarski, "Ahanakht of Bersheh," in *Studies in Anc. Eg.*, pp. 22–23 and 25, fig. 13; cf. Willems, *Chests of Life*, pp. 74–75.

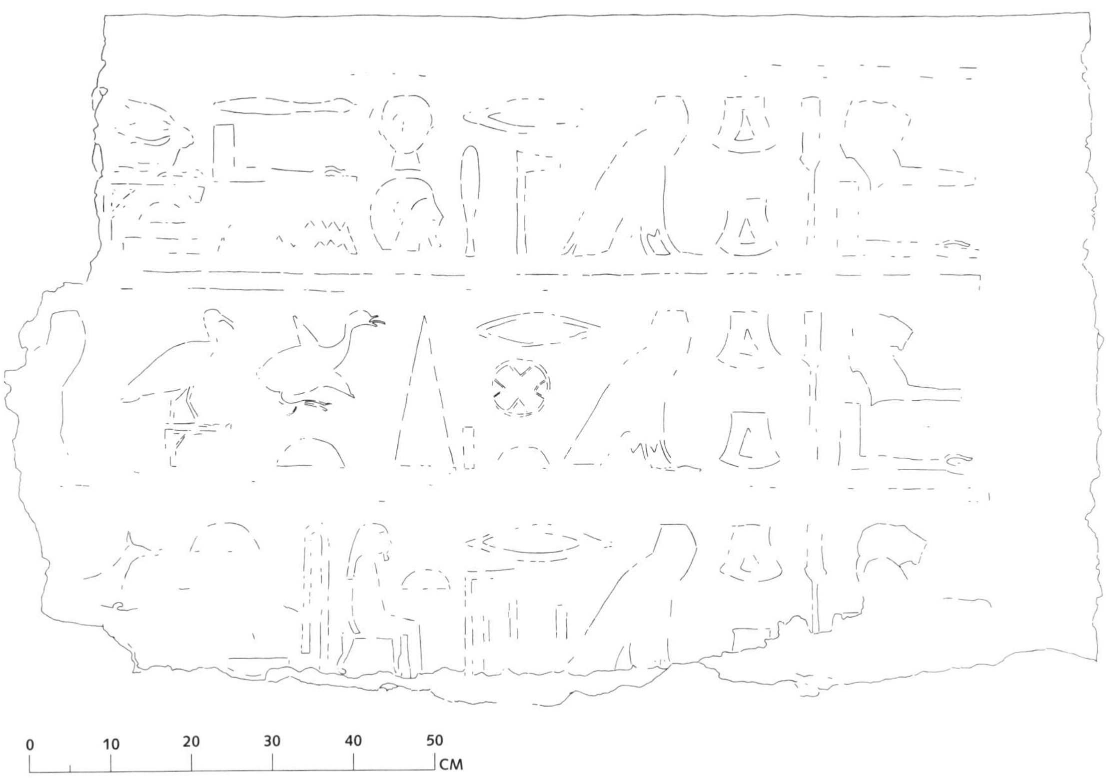

Fig. 28. Fallen lintel block from Tomb 18 with titles of the owner, probably the nomarch Amenemhat.

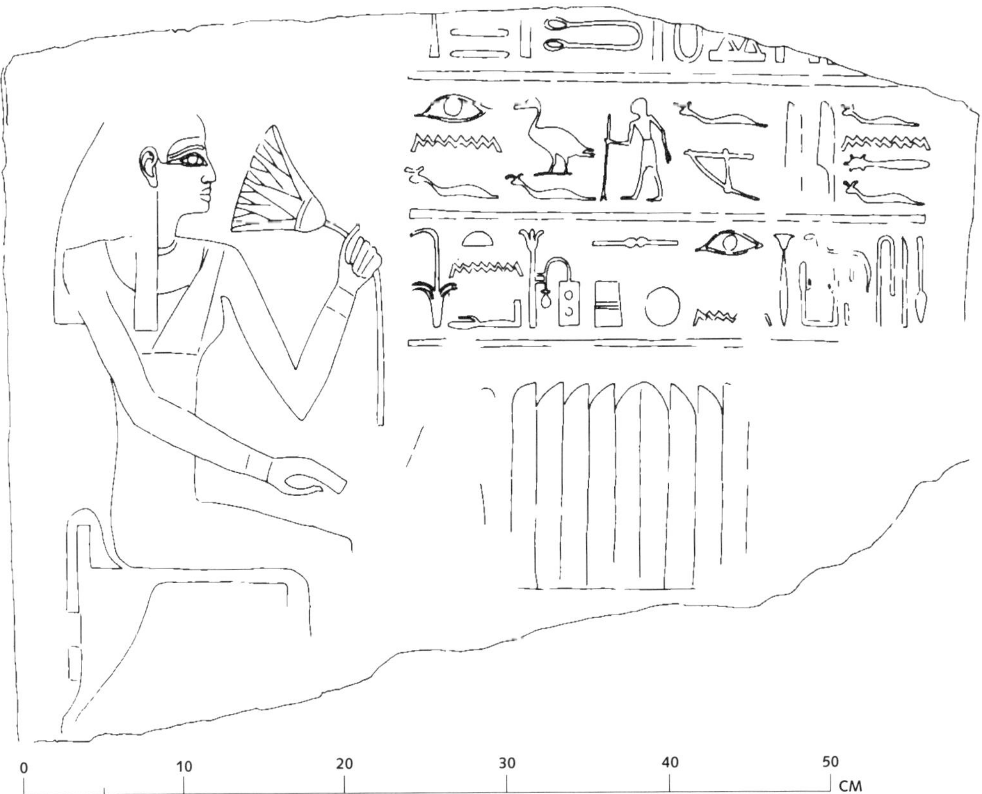

Fig. 29. Relief from Tomb 18 mentioning the name of Sep, son of Amenemhat and Wadjkaues. MFA 1972.984.

of which are largely destroyed.[46] Only fragments of the north and east walls of the outer chamber remain in situ, the rest having been quarried away.[47] In the middle of the back wall is a door leading into the inner chamber, roughly the same size as the first, but with the roof fallen in. Although the walls of the inner chamber had been dressed and plastered, they apparently never bore any decoration. The walls of the outer room, however, were carved in sunk relief and painted.

The outer chamber of Tomb 19 contains two deep shafts, both of which Reisner cleared. In the chamber of Pit B to the right, Reisner found fragments of a wooden coffin belonging to a certain Ahanakht, presumably a male relative of Nehri's, the interior of which was inscribed with incised and painted Coffin Texts.[48] On the east side of the inner chamber is another large shaft, which has been plundered. The presence of a fourth shaft alongside it is likely.

Several of the reliefs from this tomb could be identified from among those published by Newberry, including Nos. 1, 3, and 7.[49] Unhappily, the scene of wrestlers on No. 7, which originally formed the north wall of the outer room to the east of the doorway, has been completely destroyed by vandals at some point after it was copied by the Egypt Exploration Fund and photographed by Reisner (see fig. 53).[50] Only the animals which form part of a hunt scene at the top of the same block have survived.

No. 3 still formed part of the inner right hand wall of the tomb when Newberry and Griffith visited Bersheh. The present expedition found the lower portion of the relief, with the word *ỉ3dt*, "net," the phrase *ỉn mrt=f n ḏt=f*, and the lower part of Nehri's face, his forearm, fist, and part of his staff face down, firmly wedged beneath a huge boulder which had broken free since the 1890's and fallen on the intact wall. In an adjacent tomb, Tomb 9, was discovered the upper part of the relief, with a *kheker* frieze, block border, the top of Nehri's head, and the words *[Nḥr]ỉ ms.n Kmỉ*, broken off undoubtedly by the impact of the fallen stone. The colors are well preserved, especially on the lower portion which shows bright blue hieroglyphs on a creamy white ground, while the color of Nehri's skin is a clear red. The *kheker* ornaments are light green, and the block border and hieroglyphs below bright blue.

Two large fragments with scenes of plowing, harvesting flax, and netting birds, not published by Newberry and Griffith, but which clearly belong to Tomb 19 on stylistic grounds, rest on the terrace just in front of the tomb (fig. 30). The first fits on top of the second, and together they form a section roughly six feet square (c. 78 x 74 cm). Taking into account the bird netting scene on the lower fragment with the caption *sḫt [ỉ]3dt nt 3pdw*, "closing the bird net," and the mention of the word *ỉ3dt*, "bird net," on No. 3 above, it seems likely that the two fragments on the terrace formed the outer half of the right-hand wall of the tomb, with the standing figure of Nehri I on No. 3 on the left, looking outwards. At the lower left the Seal-bearer Nemty-em-hat and another individual bring birds for the *ka* of Nehri.

Newberry describes, but does not illustrate a relief on the west side of the doorway to the inner chamber with fragments of figures of Nehri I standing, accompanied by a woman of equal height, presumably his wife, Djehutynakht (fig. 31).[51] The pair are approached by an attendant who leads an ox. During this season, an additional fragment of relief with the upper part of the figures was found on the talus slope in front of Tomb 19 (See figs. 3 and 31). It was retrieved, temporarily returned to its proper place, drawn, and photographed. The expedition also recovered several other broken reliefs in the course of a brief reconnaissance. The inference to be drawn from the location of the discoveries is that earlier excavators, intent on excavating the tomb shafts and burials, simply tipped the fill from the tombs over the cliff edge.

E. Reisner 21 – The Tomb of Djehutynakht

1. Physical Description

This tomb is located at the north-westernmost end of the terrace. It is flanked on the northwest by a quarry and on the south-east by the tomb of Djehutyhotep. The surface in this area is very

45. R. Anthes, *Die Felseninschriften von Hatnub*, Graffiti nos. 14–24.
46. *El Bersheh* II, pl. X.
47. Ibid., p. 27 and pl. X.
48. Obj. Reg. 15–5–638; the fragments are now in Boston.
49. Ibid., pl. XI.
50. Cf. EEF fragment No. 7, mentioned in the text (ibid., p. 29) and reproduced on pl. XI.
51. Ibid., p. 29.

Fig. 30. Scenes of plowing, harvesting flax, and netting birds from the tomb of Nehri I, Tomb 19.

Fig. 31. Damaged scene of Nehri I and his wife on the back wall of the outer chamber to the left of the entrance to the inner chamber of Tomb 19.

Fig. 32. View of Tomb 21, the tomb of Djehutynakht VI, looking southeast, with the shrine visible at right.

uneven; strewn with boulders, smaller rock, gravel, and spoil heaps from previous excavations and possibly ancient quarrying (fig. 32). When the ceiling collapsed into the tomb, the walls were unable to withstand the force of collapse and shattered. While many fragments fell into the tomb, and some were undoubtedly ground to dust by the collapsed ceiling, numerous others remain more or less in situ.

The staff made a preliminary plan (fig. 33) to aid in the identification of important features. This divided the vicinity of this tomb into 5.0 meter squares;[52] each has been labelled alphabetically, left to right and rear to front. All references in the subsequent paragraphs refer to this plan.

The two squares (I and J) at the front are occupied primarily by spoil. The large boulder in squares H and K is inscribed and decorated on its underside, and was formerly part of the ceiling of the tomb. The tourist path which gives access to this tomb runs along the crest of the spoil heaps in squares I, J, and K at the front, then back along the left side of the tomb area through squares G and D, and into the interior of the tomb at two points: one in squares A and B, and one in square H.

The surface of the tourist path consists of limestone dust, gravel, and some larger stones. Occasionally, small pieces of painted plaster and stone are visible beside the path. The inscribed fragment on the right side of the path in square G was

52. This grid was constructed by triangulation using metric tapes. In some cases the terrain made it exceedingly difficult to make accurate measurements. Therefore, this plan has an error factor of +/– 0.50 meters per 5.0 meter square. Also, the instability of the surface around the shafts and the physical obstacle of the collapsed ceiling made it impossible to obtain exact measurements for the length of the right wall from rear to front. Therefore, the location of the rear of the tomb in squares A and B is approximate in relation to features in the other squares. The dimensions given on the plan for the left, rear, and right walls (where accessible) are accurate. In future seasons, a surveyor will generate a more accurate map.

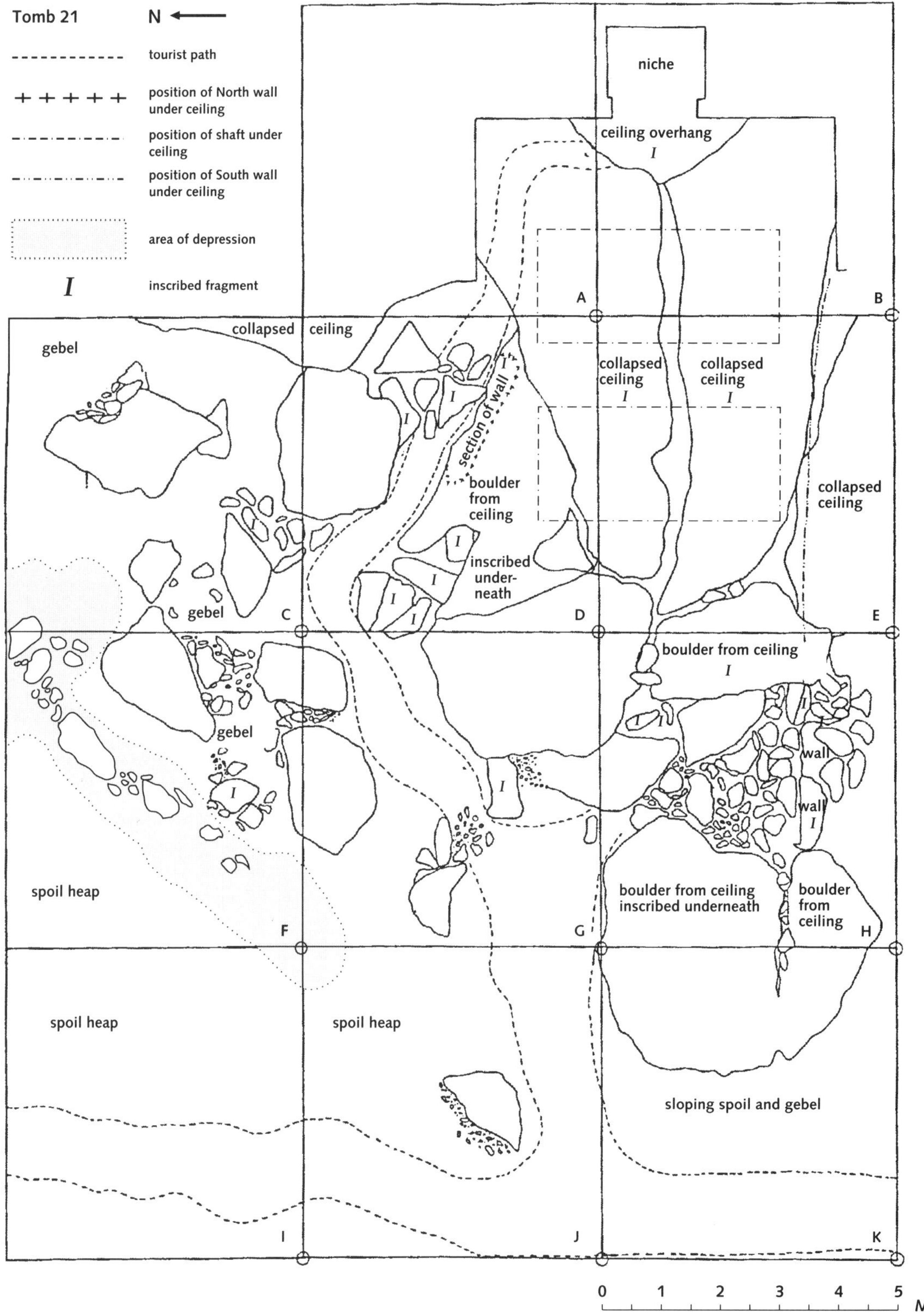

Fig. 33. Preliminary plan of Tomb 21.

Fig. 34. View of the collapsed ceiling and rear shaft of Tomb 21 with a decorated fragment of relief from the right-hand wall wedged under the ceiling block.

formerly part of the left wall. The forces that destroyed the tomb were so intense that it was flipped upside down and reversed, with the result that its inscribed surface now faces outward. The large boulder to the rear that partially covers this fragment was part of the ceiling.

A large depression is located where squares F, G, I, and J meet. It is formed by the meeting of the spoil heaps and debris from the tomb. Crossing square F on a diagonal, this depression continues into square C. Square D contains several fragments from the left wall of the tomb. The fragment beneath the large ceiling boulder is in situ, and decoration and inscription remain on its inner side.

Squares A, B, D, E, G and H are dominated by large boulders from the collapsed ceiling. Two very large "triangular" boulders are wedged point down into the shafts and block the surrounding area (fig. 34). It was deemed too hazardous to obtain dimensions for the shafts or to measure the shafts with relation to the tomb wall this season; only the approximate location of the shafts is sketched on the plan.[53]

2. *Epigraphic Work*

Tomb 21, the burial place of Djehutynakht VI, governor of the Hare nome under Amenemhat I or Sesostris I, is much ruined by earthquake and quarrying.[54] It is large, but evidently consists only of a single, oblong chamber with a statue shrine in the center of the rear wall.[55] Chamber and shrine were completely decorated in paint or in painted sunk relief. The shrine contained a seated statue of Djehutynakht cut in the rock, but this has been

53. The measurements used for drawing the shafts in the plan (fig. 12) are those given in *El Bersheh* II, pl. IV. Generally, the measurements given in the EEF publication have proven accurate to within +/− 0.10 cm.

54. On the date of Djehutynakht VI, see Brovarski, "Ahanakht of Bersheh," in *Studies in Anc. Eg.*, pp. 22–23, 25, fig. 13; see also Willems, *Chests of Life*, pp. 74–75.

badly mutilated.[56] The facade of the tomb had been entirely quarried away in antiquity. Perhaps in the aftermath of the earthquake postulated by Fraser, the side walls of the tomb fell inward, and the roof slid forward, so that its front portion now lies completely outside the tomb in squares H and K. The back portion of the roof was split up into four or five great sections and fell inside the main chamber. Both the shrine and the inner walls escaped with only slight damage.[57] The end of the south wall was also left essentially intact and was reconstructed in part on paper by Newberry from fragments found in the debris on the floor of the tomb.[58] The figure of Djehutynakht at the right end of this wall is still in place. The rest of the wall is evidently represented by the jumble of blocks that fill this area. A fragment with an inscription in large and detailed hieroglyphs, originally above the head of Djehutynakht, is now largely buried in earth and debris, perhaps in the same location where Griffith and Newberry saw it, just to the right of the tourist path in Square G (see fig. 32).[59]

A large piece of the north wall, reaching from top to bottom, is still in place at the east end. Griffith and Newberry published the texts on this wall as well as the majority of the accessible inscriptions throughout the tomb. They published only a schematic diagram of the decoration, however, which included scenes of hunting and fishing, and an elaborate depiction of Djehutynakht's funeral.[60] A depiction of the mummy on a lion-footed bier and a *tekenu* on its sledge are two previously unnoticed details on this wall. The outer end of the wall is also a tumble of blocks at present. One well-preserved fragment shows that the original background color of the scenes was a creamy white. The hieroglyphs include a finely painted newborn bubalis or hartebeast in salmon with a large black eye and red outlines. Below are bright green papyrus stalks with umbels tipped in canary yellow. Although the figure of a marsh bird perched on one umbel has lost its head and diagnostic crest, its long legs and squared tail suggest that the bird might be a lapwing.[61] A second fragment bears the beginning of a caption, *ḫns,* "traversing (by boat)..." The decoration on these fragments suggests the motif of a marsh scene. Considering that a fishing scene occurs on the rear wall to the left of the shrine, perhaps the representation at the outer end of the left-hand wall portrayed Djehutynakht fowling.

Although Griffith and Newberry again published the texts, they did not include descriptions or drawings of the representations on the east wall to either side of the statue shrine. The wall to the left of the shrine depicts a large scale fishing scene with figures of Djehutynakht and his wife Hathorhetep in a papyrus skiff in sunk relief. The scene on the wall to the right of the shrine is especially interesting. It consists of the standing figure of a vizier on the right, accompanied by a woman standing behind him. The vizier faces left towards four men who approach and present to him different shaped boxes, containing incense and other precious substances. His titles are inscribed in columns above his head but the name, unfortunately, is lost.[62] It is possible that he is the brother of Djehutynakht, Amenemhat, who has the titles of vizier on the fallen architrave in front of Tomb 3 (fig. 28).[63]

Beneath his feet is a register occupied by quarrymen. The superscription reads: *wpt ḥwtt wḫꜣ ỉnr ỉn [ṯzwt] n ḫrtyw-nṯr n ḥꜣty-ꜥ Ḏḥwty-nḫt,* "Opening a gallery and hewing stone by the [crews] of quarrymen for the count Djehutynakht."[64] The quarrymen, bent double over a block of stone, raise their mallets above their heads so as to strike the chisels in their other hand with greater force. To the left is an intricately composed scene (fig. 35). From the lower right hand corner of the composition, a double line rises at an acute angle. On the left end of the incline formed by the diagonal lines sits a quarryman. Facing him is a companion who stands on the diagonal and whose forward hand he grasps with his own left hand. Below and a little behind the

55. Both Tomb 21 and Tomb 1, the tomb of Djehutynakht's father, Nehri II, evidently consisted of a single chamber. In the tomb of Nehri II a sloping shaft, rabbeted so as to be closed with a stone slab, opens in the center of the rear wall, instead of the shrine as in Tomb 21. In contrast, the earlier tombs of Ahanakht I (Tomb 5) and Nehri I (Tomb 19) were composed of two chambers without a shrine; see, *El Bersheh* II, pp. 29, 30ff., pls. X and XII; Terrace, *Egyptian Paintings,* p. 12; cf. Brovarski, "Ahanakht of Bersheh," in *Studies in Anc. Eg.*, p. 22, n. 53.

56. *El Bersheh* II, p. 58, pl. IV.

57. G.W. Fraser, in ibid., p. 58.

58. Ibid., pl. VIII.

59. Ibid., p. 19; above, pp. 34–35.

60. Ibid., p. 18.

61. See Patrick F. Houlihan, *The Birds of Ancient Egypt,* pp. 93–96, no. 48.

62. *El Bersheh* II, p. 24.

63. See Brovarski, "Ahanakht of Bersheh," in *Studies in Anc. Eg.*, p. 23 and n. 60.

64. *El Bersheh* II, p. 24.

Fig. 35. Preliminary rendering of scene on the right-hand side of the east (rear) wall in Tomb 21.

seated figure is a man standing on the groundline of the register who raises his arm above his head to hold the seated man's right hand. Beside the standing man is a slightly stooped figure with both hands on the diagonal. A third figure kneels on the ground and stretches his rear leg out. His head is in the angle formed by the diagonal and the groundline, and he turns his face upwards. The significance of this scene is not immediately apparent. It is possible that a construction ramp or incline is represented, but several points argue against this possibility. The double diagonal appears to terminate in midair, and although the surface is relatively well-preserved, no vertical line is visible to complete the outline of a ramp. In addition, the hands of the two figures on the groundline intersect the diagonal lines and seem to grasp them. It is likely that the raised hand of the third figure also held on to the diagonal lines.

It should be emphasized that the drawing in fig. 35, traced from a photograph made under difficult conditions, is not collated and many details remain to be confirmed.[65] It is possible, however, to suggest another interpretation. The three workmen shown raise a long pole (perhaps part of a scaffold) to which their two comrades cling. The accompanying caption (only partially visible in fig. 35) might clarify what was going on, if its own import were clearer: *smn tw pr.ti r mꜣḥy*, "Be steady as you go (up?) to the *mꜣḥy*!"[66]

The ceiling of Djehutynakht's tomb was richly ornamented. The great ceiling blocks that now fill

65. Thanks are due Peter Der Manuelian for the preliminary drawing reproduced here as fig. 35.

66. The writer has benefitted from discussions about the texts accompanying the scenes with Drs. James P. Allen, David P. Silverman and Edward F. Wente and would like to thank them for their interest and ideas. In the course of the Sixth International Congress of Egyptology at Turin in September 1991, Mr. T.G.H. James made the alternative suggestion that the workmen are using a pole as a lever. If this alternative is accepted, the inscription might be rendered differently.

most of its interior are painted in bright colors on their undersides with a checker pattern of small squares, each containing a quatrefoil. The long columns of blue-painted funerary texts on the ceiling are similar to those in the tomb of his father, Nehri II (Tomb 1).[67]

Two large transverse mummy-pits lie across the axis of Tomb 21. The Egypt Exploration Fund was unable to clear the front shaft in 1891–1892, as the great mass of the fallen roof lay above it, and Griffith and Newberry evidently were unaware of the existence of the shaft at the rear of the chamber.[68] Both mummy-pits, like all the shafts and chambers on the terrace, will have to be re-excavated in order to determine whether or not they were completely emptied by earlier excavators. We do know Fraser reburied the pottery he found at the tombs. The same is true of the relief fragments found by him which were not taken to the British Museum or assigned to other collections.[69]

The wall surfaces throughout the tomb were overlaid with a thin coat of plaster in which the scenes and inscriptions were carved in a shallow sunk relief. In places this layer of plaster is now badly cracked and peeling. The friable nature of some of the surfaces mandates the use of photography for the recording of the decoration in many instances. The great sections of fallen roof, the debris that partially fills the chamber and shrine, and the gaping shafts, however, complicated the process of photographing the scenes and inscriptions in the tomb and the staff was therefore unable to make a complete photographic record this year. In future seasons, the chamber and shrine will be cleared to floor level to facilitate the recording of the decoration on the walls.

67. During the 1990 season, Brian Muhs drew a preliminary reconstruction of the ceiling incorporating the fragments of texts published in *El Bersheh* II, pl. VI; see fig. 22 of the present article and the remarks made above in the article by David P. Silverman on the tomb of Nehri II (pp. 15–17).

68. *El Bersheh* II, p. 58.

69. Ibid., pp. 65–66.

CHAPTER III

TOMBS IN THE MIDDLE OF THE TERRACE

Olaf Kaper

René van Walsem

Harco Willems

A. Introduction

After the promising results of a first study visit in late 1988 to Bersheh, the Department of Egyptology of Leiden University received a concession for epigraphic field-work covering the area around Tomb 5 of Ahanakht I.[70] Attention was focused on Tomb 5 itself and on Tombs 102 and 104.[71] Preliminary research showed that the publication of Newberry and Griffith could no longer be considered adequate. The value of the copies of several reliefs and inscriptions is seriously impaired by many errors, as well as by omissions of some areas of the decoration. It is probable that some of these areas were inaccessible at the end of the last century, but in other cases, the reasons for the errors and omissions are less easy to understand.

During the expedition, the Dutch team members each worked in one of the tombs. Their reports will follow below. The season also gave an opportunity to acquire a better understanding of the archaeological history of the site.

B. The Archaeological History of the Northern Wadi Slope

The Dutch concession is situated on the north slope of the Wadi Deir en-Nakhleh, and covers two levels. The upper level is part of the rock plateau where the nomarchs' tombs of the Middle Kingdom are situated. Tomb 5, which once belonged to the nomarch Ahanakht I, is the largest in the immediate area, and it forms the center of the Dutch sector. Immediately west of this sepulchre, and on the same level, are the scant remains of the tomb of another nomarch, which we discovered in 1988.[72] This tomb has received the provisional code "Tomb X." Directly in front of Tomb 5, but on a lower level, are the tombs of three subordinates of Ahanakht I.

The nomarchal tombs were hewn out in a stratum of good quality limestone, which made them an attractive target for the quarrymen who exploited the area in the Late Period. Since the lower tombs were cut in rock of poorer quality, they have survived in a much better state of preservation. The first quarrying near the nomarchs' tombs appears to have taken place in the 18th Dynasty, witness a stela of Thutmosis III.[73] It has not been possible yet to determine whether the quarrymen already worked at that time inside the tombs themselves. Some of the quarry-marks on the roofs of the sepulchres, however, are characteristic of the Late Period, and thus testify to activity during that period.

The north slope of the wadi is covered with spoil heaps. The surface of these heaps consists of what is obviously archaeological dump. Directly to the west of Tombs 102, 103, and 104, however, the steep side of the dump reveals a profile characteristic of a quarry dump.[74] The dump at this point has a height of approximately two meters and a half, and consists of small limestone chips and chalk. The texture of this deposit is strongly reminiscent of the dumps found throughout the site, as well as inside, and near the mouths of limestone quarries.

In the Dutch sector, the entrance to the quarry appears to have been through Tomb X, of which the facade and interior were almost entirely removed. This situation explains why the quarry dump begins in front of this tomb and extends in a westerly direction. In front of Tomb 5, the surface of the dump falls off sharply, thus revealing the facades of Tombs 102–104. The area seems never to have been used intensively as a dump, although erosion must have caused the spread of spoil from the heaps in front of Tomb X.

The situation, as it can be observed nowadays, does not differ much from the one encountered in 1891–92 (fig. 36).[75] A horizontal discoloration visible on the interior walls of Tomb 104 suggests that the tomb was once filled with rubble to the

70. See Willems, "Deir el-Bersheh, Preliminary Report," *GM* 110 (1989), pp. 75–95.

71. According to the numbering introduced by the Egypt Exploration Fund (EEF) team in 1891/2, the tomb numbers are 5, 8 and 10 respectively (*El Bersheh* II). See also table in fig. 8, p. 9 in this volume.

72. See the plan published in Willems, "Deir el-Bersheh," *GM* 110 (1989), p. 91. In the preliminary report, it was suggested that the owner may be Ahanakht II, the son of Ahanakht I. An inscribed stone found since in the debris of the tomb contains the word *ꜥḥꜣ* which may be part of the name.

73. Its position can be inferred from the plan published by Griffith and Newberry (*El Bersheh* II, pl. II). On the other side of the wadi exists a second stela erected by Amenhotep III, see above, n. 2.

74. The archaeological dump, which also consists of an important amount of quarry debris, is interspersed with pebbles and larger stone blocks, as well as with pottery and wood fragments. The volume of the archaeological dumps must be considerable. Some of Reisner's field photographs, made at the beginning of his 1915 excavation, show that the plateau was then still covered with thick deposits of debris.

75. See Willems, "Deir el-Bersheh," *GM* 110 (1989), p. 92, fig. 9.

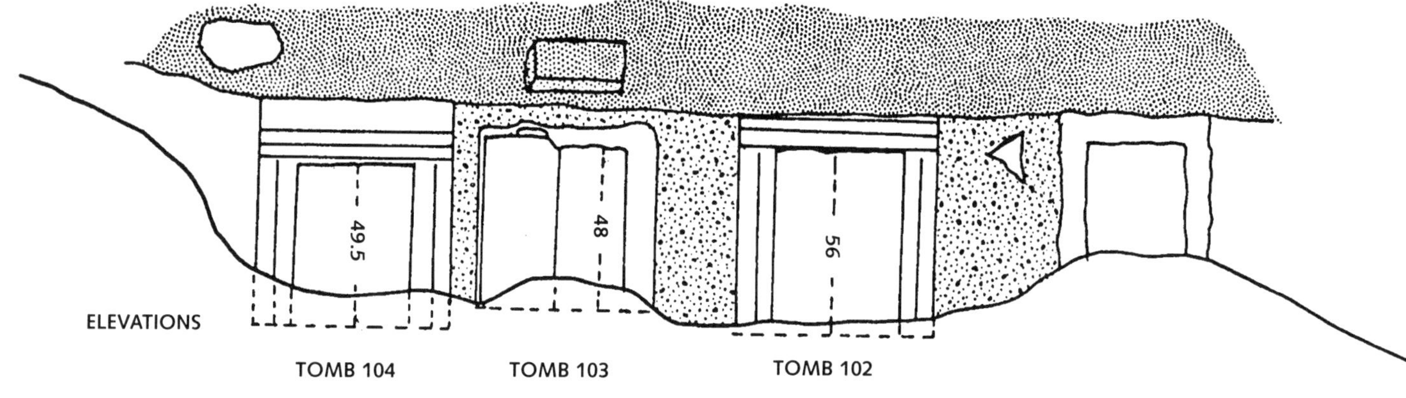

Fig. 36. View of the facades of Tombs 102–104 (right to left). The quarry dump is indicated to the left of Tomb 104 (cf. *El Bersheh* II, pl. XX). Measurements are given in centimeters.

Fig. 37. Harvard - BMFA Expedition photograph (no. C 6798) showing part of the facade of Tomb 5 (the sharp rock edge to the left), the terrace in front of the tomb, and the dump to the far right. The trench in the middle shows the entrances to Tombs 102–104 (the three farthest ones) and several others. The limestone slab blocking the entrance to Tomb 103 (see fig. 36) is shown still in situ.

discoloration level—a much lower level than the top of the spoil-heaps to the west. There are no indications that Tombs 102–103, which are further removed from the dump, were ever filled with rubble. It is not irrelevant here to note the later use of tomb 102 as a shelter or a kitchen (see van Walsem's contribution).

These observations are more interesting than they may at first seem. The area in front of Tomb 5 is one of the few places where the slope of the wadi is hardly covered with deposits of quarry dump, but, at this point, a group of tombs (102–104) immediately emerges from under the rubble. A trench dug through the dump by one of our predecessors, probably Reisner (fig. 37), revealed a further series

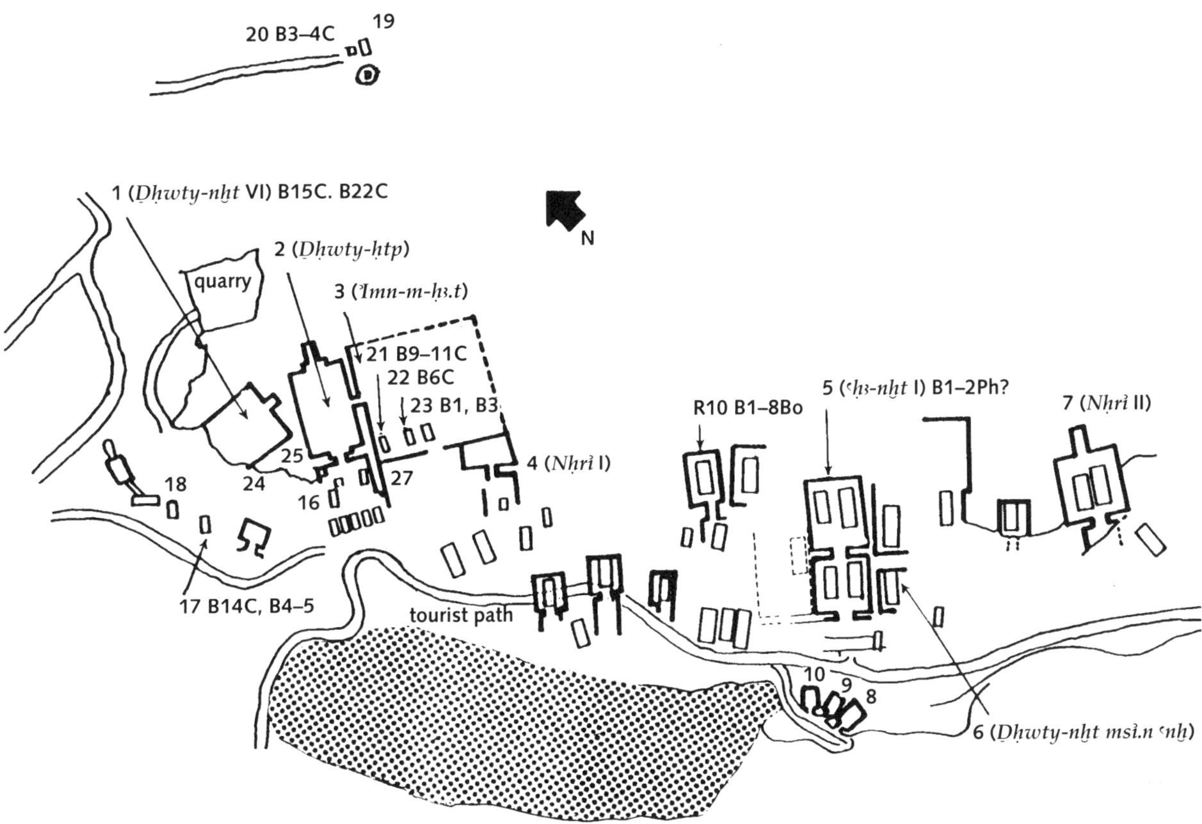

Fig. 38. Sketch of the Middle Kingdom cemetery. The hatched area indicates the approximate position of the quarry dump on the north wadi slope, which may cover a Middle Kingdom cemetery.

of tombs extending in a northwesterly direction. Much further to the northwest, as one climbs the hill to the plateau of nomarchs' tombs, one can see traces of additional tombs partially covered with quarry dump at a much lower level. This observation suggests that the quarry dump covers a Middle Kingdom cemetery of subordinates of the nomarchs buried in the upper plateau (fig. 38). Since extensive dumps also exist in the area in front of Tombs 20 and 21, a similar cemetery may occur there.

C. Tomb 5 – The Tomb of Ahanakht

This tomb was initially published by Griffith and Newberry, but a recording of the outer chamber made in this first season by the present author allows a new introduction to the nature of the decoration to be presented.[76] The following remarks are intended to replace the previously published description of the tomb.

Tomb 5 consists of two connected rock-cut chambers, and five shafts, one of which actually lies outside the monument. The two chambers are roughly rectangular; the first, although somewhat smaller than the second, has a higher ceiling (fig. 39). The five shafts were numbered A–E by Reisner in 1915; two are cut in the floor of each chamber, and one smaller shaft lies in front of the tomb. The walls of the two chambers of the tomb were entirely decorated with carved and painted reliefs, with two false door-stelae situated on the left wall of the inner chamber. Most of the walls are now badly damaged and many parts of them are completely destroyed.

Some of the destruction in the tomb is due to quarrying that took place in the later periods of Egyptian history. However, such activity may have occurred already by the New Kingdom, as evidenced by a stela from the time of Thutmosis III in

[76] *El Bersheh* II, pp. 30–35 and pls. XII–XVII.

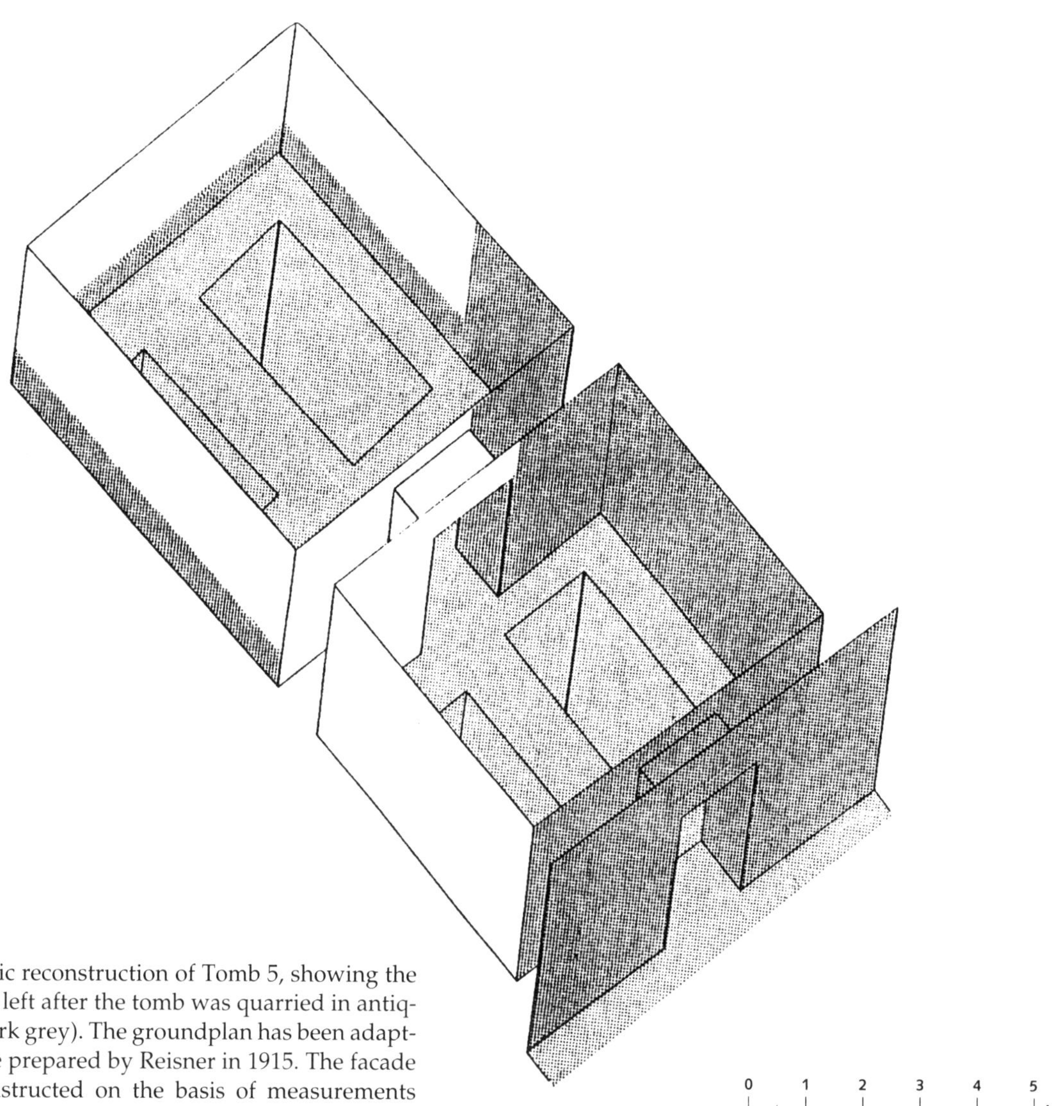

Fig. 39. Isometric reconstruction of Tomb 5, showing the walls that were left after the tomb was quarried in antiquity (shaded dark grey). The groundplan has been adapted from the one prepared by Reisner in 1915. The facade has been reconstructed on the basis of measurements taken from fragments lying in front of the tomb.

a neighboring quarry.[77] Not only were the walls quarried, but the ceiling of the tomb as well, and only fragments of it are left now. Figure 39 shows how little of the walls was left after the quarrying. A group of incised graffiti in the first chamber showing animals and a human figure may well have been made by men working in these quarries; similar figures in paint are found elsewhere in the area. As a result of the extensive quarrying of stone, the mountain collapsed probably not long afterwards, causing the front of the tomb to tumble down and preventing access to the inner chamber. Sometime thereafter, a Coptic cenobitic community settled in the quarries and in the remaining tombs. It is not clear as to whether they or their predecessors were responsible for damaging the figure of a griffin in the first chamber. Acting out of fear of the magical potential of the decoration, the Coptic monks may have been the ones responsible for damage to the scenes and texts as well as for the painting of a series of crosses in red paint in all the accessible parts of the tomb. In a later attempt to obliterate the traces of the Coptic presence in the area, others hacked out the crosses. Finally, in the nineteenth and twentieth centuries, looters sawed out a number of fragments of the reliefs. A similar

77. Ibid., n. 2 and p. 62; see also Robinson, p. 3, n. 2 in this volume.

chronology of destruction can be observed in the other tombs at Bersheh.

Despite such devastation, some decoration in Tomb 5 has survived fairly well, notably that in the inner chamber, owing to the fact that it was filled with debris from natural disasters for half its history. Fortunately, enough remains to allow conclusions to be made in regard to the original appearance of most of the walls. In fact, of all two-room tombs in the Bersheh necropolis, the tomb of Ahanakht has survived the best. This fact is important for there may have been a series of tombs with a similar ground-plan in the area around Tomb 5, all of which are now in fragmentary condition. This situation makes Tomb 5 an important model for the study of the less well-preserved tombs of its type.

The front of the tomb has completely collapsed, blocking the original entrance. The reconstruction presented in figure 39 has been made from measurements taken from the various remaining fragments. The original width of the facade was about 6.60 meters and its height more than 2.85 meters. Its decoration consisted of a large biographical text of 23 vertical lines of inscription. Twelve lines were carved on the left-hand side of the entrance and eleven lines on the right, all in blue-painted hieroglyphs. Over the door was a horizontal text of four lines containing an offering formula and the names and titles of the tomb owners, the foremost of whom was Ahanakht. Griffith and Newberry included in their reconstruction of the facade some fragments of jamb inscriptions, three lines in width. In their drawing, however, the orientation of the signs does not conform to the usual direction of this kind of inscription.[78] Since no such fragments have survived today, we cannot check them against the copy.

The thickness of the doorway on either side shows a large figure of the deceased facing out of the tomb, and a column of hieroglyphs containing his name and titles is written in front of him. The same decoration is found on the second doorway leading to the inner chamber.

The two chambers share the following elements in their iconography. In each chamber, columns are depicted in the corners of the side walls, lotus columns in the first and papyrus columns in the second. Each column spans almost the entire height of the wall, and each is isolated from the other decoration of the chamber, as if they were actual architectural features of the tomb. Apparently, the two chambers were thought to represent the south and the north, a supposition that is supported by the positioning of the offering place, which is associated with the west, in the west wall of the inner chamber. Actually, the direction of the tomb presents a divergence from the magnetic north of about 35 degrees. The significance of this apparent division of the rooms between north and south remains to be established.[79]

In between the columns on the walls, the various scenes are grouped within vertical bands colored from top to bottom alternating red-blue-yellow-green, each framed within blue lines. The scenes themselves are cut in shallow incised relief, while these bands are only painted. The tomb has no *kheker* pattern, but instead, a series of horizontal bands painted in the colors mentioned above marks the upper border of the scenes. These bands number either five or three in those places where they are preserved, but they are in most cases destroyed.

Only fragments remain of the ceiling. The ceiling in the outer chamber had a painted yellow ground with blue stars with yellow centers in relief each about 0.20 meters in width. The stars are laid out regularly in rows. The ceiling is bordered by a thick red-painted line which measures more than 0.20 meters in width. The inner chamber, however, has so little of its ceiling preserved that none of the stars and only traces of the red lines remain.

Yellow is also found as a background color on the walls; the hieroglyphs are painted blue. It seems that all the scenes in the tomb were crowned by a double line of hieroglyphs giving the name and titles of Ahanakht and offering formulae. The hieroglyphs in these lines were drawn with the use of red guidelines, similar to those of the artists working in Tombs 102 and 104.

A distinctive aspect of the decoration of Tomb 5 is the orientation of the scenes on the walls. Only the double line of hieroglyphs over the scenes follows the usual practice of directing the representations and their texts in relation to the offering place. The scenes below the lines of hieroglyphs, however, often show a reversal of this order, where the tomb owner is facing towards the back of the tomb,

78. *El Bersheh* II, p. 33 and pls. XII (front elevation) and XIII.

79. See the suggestions made by Rita E. Freed, p. 56 in this volume. See also Brovarski, "Ahanakht of Bersheh," in *Studies in Anc. Eg.*, pp. 14–17, n. 7, with figs. 4 (lotiform capital missing) and 6 (papyriform capital).

in the direction of the offering place. The reason for this practice is not clear, but parallels occur in the contemporaneous Tombs 102 and 104. The scenes in the thicknesses of the doorways conform again to the usual order, as the figures of the deceased here face the entrance of the tomb.

Thematically, the decoration in the first chamber of Tomb 5 is characterized by the provision of offerings. The west wall has been completely quarried away and nothing more than a few lines of the lotus columns in the corners remain, but the decoration on the other walls may be reconstructed to a great extent. The bottom register portrays a series of marsh scenes, showing a large fish-net, cattle crossing water, a bird-netting scene, and a scene showing some birds in the water.[80] The respective registers immediately above depict these categories of animals carried as offerings to the deceased. The scenes show rows of men bringing fish, meat, and poultry before Ahanakht, who was probably depicted seated in the right corner of the right sidewall. Only his name is preserved here, the remainder of the wall having been quarried. The figure probably would have looked towards the interior of the tomb, judging from the orientation of the hieroglyphs of his name, as well as from direction of the offering bearers walking towards him.

Another figure of the deceased seated in front of an offering table is found on the south wall of the first chamber, next to (west of) the original doorway. He was originally accompanied by a row of eight dancers of which only a few legs remain today. On the east side of the doorway, the same wall has a relief depicting a donkey being led and the remains of what probably was a hunting scene. Traces of two smaller portraits of Ahanakht in the first chamber are found on either side of the inner doorway at the bottom of two jamb inscriptions.[81] These standing figures are part of the inscriptions above, since they function as a large determinative for his name;[82] they face towards the door, as is usual. It is possible that similar figures adorned the jambs of the outer doorway. Other scenes preserved in the first chamber include a procession of fantastic and exotic animals on the rear wall, among others, a griffin and a deer. The upper registers of the east wall are covered with a series of small, kneeling offering-bearers who are part of an extensive offering list displayed in several registers.

Since the walls of the inner chamber are preserved only to a low height, except in one corner, only the scenes at the bottom remain for the most part. On the west wall the false doors were carved in extremely deep relief similar to that in the contemporaneous Tombs 102 and 104. They preserve the names of Ahanakht and Djehutynakht. Between these two false doors is a scene of a bull-fight, a theme repeated elsewhere in the same chamber.[83] On the right side of the false doors are three small registers depicting dogs[84] and part of an object frieze with some chests and a collection of different tools. On the bottom of the north wall of the room is an aquatic scene. Parts of four boats between papyrus plants are preserved. The boats are rowed toward the right, away from the false doors. The scene on the east wall is a parallel to that on the same wall in the outer chamber. It preserves on the right side the seated figure of Ahanakht before an offering table,[85] and on the left a row of eighteen offering-bearers forming part of an offering list. Finally, the south wall to the east of the doorway carries a virtually undamaged scene showing Ahanakht and four other men receiving two branches of the moringa tree, an offering which is not uncommon in Bersheh (see p. 62). Below, two registers show herding scenes with cows and bulls in separate registers.[86]

The preserved scenes in the tomb are only in a few cases provided with explanatory texts. Sometimes these inscriptions are given the form of a third line of larger hieroglyphs at the top of the wall, and only in one case, on the north wall of the outer chamber, do they appear as glosses in small hieroglyphs with the scenes themselves. Other scenes have no textual explanation at all.

Griffith and Newberry's publication provides drawings of only parts of the scenes in the first chamber and of the well-preserved right (east) wall of the second chamber. The inner chamber probably had not been completely cleared, with the result that their drawings are often sketchy, and large

80. Ibid., pp. 14 and 16 (fig. 4).

81. Ibid., pp. 14 and 16 (fig. 5).

82. Henry G. Fischer, "Redundant Determinatives in the Old Kingdom," *MMJ* 8 (1973): 7–25.

83. Brovarski, "Ahanakht of Bersheh," in *Studies in Anc. Eg.*, pp. 16 and 17 (figs. 7 and 8), and 11.

84. Perhaps instead of the "fabulous creatures" as suggested in ibid., pp. 16 and 20 (fig. 9).

85. Ibid., pp. 16 and 17 (fig. 6).

86. Ibid., pp. 15 (fig. 2) and 16.

sections of some scenes have been misplaced or simply omitted. Although they included a drawing of two registers of cattle on plate XIV, this scene actually belongs to the drawing on plate XVII.[87] Despite these problems, the recordings of Griffith and Newberry preserve the appearance of several fragments which have been sawn out or have simply disappeared since the end of the last century.

D. Tomb 102 – The tomb of Iha

The present author carried out work of a mainly epigraphic nature in Reisner 102 (EEF 8), the tomb of Iha. Tomb 102 was first published by Sayce and then by Griffith and Newberry prior to this century.[88] Our first season confirmed that the publications of this tomb were not completely accurate. The previous descriptions of the tomb indicated considerable damage, but our survey noticed less than that reported. The publication pretends at a higher degree of accuracy for the published texts than we could justify during our recent epigraphic work.

On the exterior of the tomb, framing the entrance are two horizontal lines of text above and two columns of texts on both sides. Many of the lacunae in the published version of the texts could be restored after we examined the partly damaged inscriptions under different light conditions over a period of several days.[89] Newberry completely overlooked the small representation of the tomb owner below the columns of inscription beside the entrance. He sits on a chair, and holds a long staff in one hand.

The interior of the tomb consists of a single oblong chamber (+/–2.00 x 2.90 meters) with a shaft (+/– 1.05 x 2.60 meters) in the middle.[90] Newberry's description of the interior contains many inaccuracies, some of which are quite baffling, since they were written by a person who had actually been to the site. This situation gives one the impression that either the field notes were inaccurate or partly lost, forcing Newberry to compose the report from memory, or alternatively, to work from the photographs of a certain Major Brown.[91] Otherwise, it is hardly explicable why only the horizontal line of text beneath the ceiling on the south inner wall is mentioned, but not the object friezes below.[92] Or how, concerning the west wall, Newberry can state at one and the same time that Sayce's sketch of the heavily damaged false door in the middle[93] is unintelligible and, a few lines below assert of the long text on both sides of the false door "... a careful copy has been made..."[94] On the spot, one can easily understand and correct Sayce's "unintelligible sketch"! The published copy of the text[95] also demonstrates that it was not taken directly from the wall; e.g., col. 1 reversal of the *mr*-sign in the original; col.7 the *m* of *ỉm* written behind the *ỉ*, col. 8 the *s* in *sbꜣ*, etc.

Newberry's description of the opposite east wall is also surprising. The reader is referred to Sayce,[96] where the texts are published, and it is unambiguously stated that below the offering list on the wall there are three bulls, each led by a man towards the offering table (with a seated figure of Iha) to the right. Newberry, however, states "... there are some traces of a scene of bulls fighting(?)..."[97] One also wonders why Newberry did not include either a copy of this wall in his publication or a reference to Sayce's copy.[98]

Finally in regard to the inscription on the rear (north) wall of the tomb,[99] Newberry states that the greater part had been damaged after 1889 and that the "remains of the original were compared with Prof. Sayce's complete copy, and the result checked by Major Brown's photograph."[100] However, the meandering line on plate XXI starts in the wrong column on the right side, viz. 2; it actually starts in col. 3, while col. 2 is completely undamaged. Apart from these mistakes, some hieroglyphs are inconsistently or inadequately rendered. Clearly, once again, Newberry's copy is not a copy made directly in front of the wall.

87. Ibid., pp. 14 and 15 (fig. 2).

88. A.-H. Sayce, "Gleanings from the land of Egypt: 3. The Tomb of [hieroglyphs] (Ahanakht) at Bersheh," *RecTrav.* 13 (1890), pp. 187–191; *El Bersheh* II, pp. 38–41, 46 and pls. XX (plan and elevation) and XXI (texts).

89. Ibid., pp. 38–39.

90. Exact measurements and orientations still have to be established by a surveyor next season.

91. Ibid., pp. 38 and 40.

92. Ibid., p. 39.

93. Sayce, "Gleanings," *RecTrav* 13, p. 190.

94. *El Bersheh* II, p. 39.

95. Ibid., pl. XXI [bottom].

96. Sayce, "Gleanings," *RecTrav.* 13, pp. 187–88.

97. *El Bersheh* II, p. 40.

98. Sayce, "Gleanings," *RecTrav.* 13, pp. 190–91.

99. *El Bersheh* II, pl. XXI [top].

100. Ibid., p. 40.

Although there is no doubt that Egyptology should be grateful to Newberry considering the short time and trying circumstances under which he had to work, this list of inaccuracies fully justifies the closer examination and republication of the tomb.

During this first season, the tomb was completely recorded, so that collating can be done next season, after which a complete publication will be undertaken. At present, only a few remarks must suffice. Apart from the damage caused by hacking out (large) areas of decoration, some parts of the tomb remain in good condition. The texts are executed in sunk relief and painted bright blue on a creamy background. Before the decoration was started, the entire surface of the limestone was covered with a thin layer of plaster that has since disappeared near the entrance and fallen from the ceiling. On this layer red guidelines were drawn, not only for the general layout, such as column dividers, but also for individual hieroglyphs. In particular the sign for *n* shows 3 to 4 such lines indicating the top and base of the two outer waves and the top and/or bottom line of the waves in between. Apart from these guidelines, the signs themselves were sketched in red as well. Concerning the method of drawing the long guide-lines, it should be noted that even though the surface of the walls is sometimes rather uneven clear lines can be seen even in the lower areas. This observation suggests that the lines were not applied by snapping a rope soaked in red paint against the wall but by using a ruler. This suggestion is supported by the fact that the lines at the top are thick and dark, whereas those at the bottom are thin and light. Moreover, it was noted at the bottom that the painter slipped at the end of the ruler two times, resulting in an effect similar to that which happens when one presses a piece of chalk too tightly against the ruler on a blackboard.

In short, a careful study of the broader details of the decoration has revealed unexpected aspects of the working procedure. Apart from this new information, we have also noticed that certain paleographic features (e.g., the 𓏠 *mn* sign as a game board on curved legs) that occur in the texts in both Tombs 102 and 104 suggest that the same artist(s) and/or workshop decorated both tombs.[101]

101. See Willems, pp. 48, 50, and Freed, p. 59 in this publication.

In the history subsequent to the pharaonic period one may infer that the tomb served as a "house" or "kitchen," since the right wall below the ceiling and the right part of the ceiling itself are covered with a black-brown layer of soot. In the corner of the short wall of the facade and the right wall, a smoke hole was cut through the thickness near the ceiling (fig. 36). Finally, the discoloring of the chisel marks shows that the damage was done in at least two stages, the last of which must be dated to +/− 1889. No Coptic crosses were found, in contrast to the situation in Tomb 5.

E. Tomb 104 – The Tomb of Djehutynakht

The workmanship and style of the decoration of Tomb 104 resembles that of Tomb 5 and particularly that of Tomb 102.[102] Whereas the paint in the latter is still in remarkably good condition, that in the present tomb has for the most part disappeared. The yellow color of the background has almost entirely peeled off the walls, except on the interior of the facade. In that location and occasionally elsewhere, one can still see the red guidelines of the artists that are also a prominent feature of Tomb 102. Only the blue, with which the hieroglyphs were filled in, is still preserved to an appreciable extent, particularly in the rear part of the chamber.

Because the limestone walls are extremely soft, porous and uneven, the artists of the tomb had to make extensive use of plaster. Today, much of this layer has weathered or fallen off, resulting in decreased legibility. Nevertheless, it has been possible to copy the text, and only a few signs or traces resist comprehension. Our work this season concentrated on the inscriptions, specifically the biographical text on the left wall.

Because the text in Tomb 104 has some of the same paleographic peculiarities as those found in the text in Tomb 102, it is likely that the same artist(s) may have decorated the two tombs.

The inscription in Tomb 104 consists of one long horizontal line (containing an offering formula) that extends over 24 columns of text.[103] A false

102. *El Bersheh* II, pp. 43–46, 63 and pl. XX. See also Freed, p. 59 below.

103. Originally published in part in *El Bersheh* II, p. 44. For the layout of the wall, cf. Willems, "Deir el-Bersheh," *GM* 110 (1989), pp. 81–82 and 95, fig. 12.

door topped by a horizontal line of inscription interrupts the biographical text in the columns just left of the middle of the wall.

The first five columns of the biography, left of the false door, contain the typical boasting remarks one expects to find in this genre, and it offers little information of intrinsic interest. Nevertheless, it is worth noting that the phraseology is exceptional, presenting a number of statements that were hitherto only known from Hatnub Graffito no. 12 (see further below).

The rest of the inscription also contains unconventional remarks, but here, no parallels seem to exist. Interpretation of the text is further hampered by the occurrence of many uncommon or unknown words, and by the subject matter, the nature of which seems to be quite exceptional. The following remarks are preliminary and are intended only to convey an idea of the importance of the text.[104]

After having stressed his knowledge and ability in lines 10–13, Djehutynakht states (line 14): "I knew the hours of the night in all its periods." Understanding of the next columns (15–17) is hampered by lacunae and the occurrence of unfamiliar words. A number of star-signs occur, and one damaged clause refers to "the end of the night." Perhaps the tomb owner is describing his role in some nocturnal activity apparently involving the celestial bodies and aiming at having knowledge of the hours of the night. Most probably, he was a star-watcher.[105] Since the few biographies of such individuals date to the Late Period, this makes the present text a most unusual document.

The tomb owner then refers to his other activities, and some of his titles are similarly unusual: *ḫrp n t*, "controller of bread," *ḥr.y-tp ḥnq.t*, "chieftain of beer" (col. 21), and particularly *ỉm.y-r ḥḥ.w ḥfn.w ḏbꜥ.w ḫꜣ.w šn.wt mḏ.ww bỉt*, "overseer of millions, hundreds of thousands, tens of thousands, thousands, hundreds, and tens of honey bread" (col. 18–19). They do show, however, that the tomb owner was responsible for the provision of bread and beer, and this impression is confirmed by the rest of the text. Therein it is apparent that the recipients of the provisions were certain production units that apparently once formed part of the provincial administration. The text mentions the "date-cake department" *ꜥ.t bnr.t*, the "slaughterhouse" *ꜥ.t ỉwf*, and the "herd department" *ꜥ.t ꜥw.t* (col. 20). A slightly damaged passage seems to mention the "mud brick department" *ꜥ.t ḏb.t* (col. 17). The tomb owner, Djehutynakht, then presents a list of the types of laborers subordinate to him, which includes "storekeepers" *ỉm.y-r s.t*, "bakers" *rtḥ.ty*, "gardeners" *kꜣn.w*, and "those attached to the (oil)-press, who make perfume" *ỉr.yw ỉꜥf ỉrỉ.w stỉ* (col. 21–22).[106]

In the last lines of his biography, Djehutynakht turns to yet another branch of activities, where he points out that he was a "chieftain of the desert, overseer of hunters, overseer of works in the necropolis" (*wꜥr.t*) and "overseer of Medjayu" (col. 23–24). The title "overseer of hunters" again refers to food production, although not necessarily for the benefit of the production units mentioned above. Possibly, the activity of the hunters must be connected with the expeditions to the desert. Conceivably, the title "chieftain of the desert-lands" *ḥr.y-tp ḫꜣs.wt* refers to activity in Hatnub (see below). Djehutynakht's statement that he was an overseer of works in the necropolis makes it clear that it was he who was responsible for the construction of the tombs in the Dutch sector.

It has been remarked above that the five first text columns of the inscription reveal a number of phraseological parallels with the beginning of Hatnub Graffito no. 12.[107] Many of the phrases are not attested elsewhere.

The analogies are probably not coincidental, since the graffito is dated to year 12 of the nomarch Ahanakht I. Djehutynakht's tomb is situated right below the tomb of this nomarch, and the latter's name occurs in the offering formulae in Tombs 102 and 104. The two texts are, therefore, contemporary. Moreover, the graffito is accompanied by a depiction of two men (Graffito no. 12a): the field scribe Khenemu-iqer and his son Djehutynakht-ankh. As the label to the first man indicates, he was son of a certain Djehutynakht. Is this the Djehutynakht who owned Tomb 104?

104. This description replaces what has been stated by Willems, "Deir el-Bersheh," *GM* 110 (1989), p. 82.

105. For a description of such duties, see Paule Posener-Kriéger, *Les archives du temple funeraire de Néferirkarê-Kakaï* (Les Papyrus d'Abousir) I, pp. 30–34.

106. The text indicates that the production of food and small commodities of various kinds was organized by the local government. This picture fits in well with what we know about Middle Kingdom Egypt as a centrally organized state; see most recently B. J. Kemp, *Ancient Egypt, Anatomy of a Civilization*, pp. 111–80.

107. *Hatnub*, pp. 28–31 and pls. 14–15.

The popularity of the name in the Hare nome should warn us against jumping to conclusions. Nevertheless, the contemporaneity of the two texts and the remarkable analogies in their formulation would seem to favor this suggestion, and there are other arguments as well. The activities of the hypothetical father and son show some correspondences. We know that the Djehutynakht who owned Tomb 104 led building projects and that he refers in this context to his title of "chieftain of desert lands." This may mean that he worked in Hatnub as did Khenemu-iqer. Moreover, Khenemu-iqer was a field-scribe, while Djehutynakht was responsible, among other things, for the gardeners. Thus both men had administrative agricultural functions.

It is, therefore, at least a distinct possibility that Hatnub Graffito no. 12 was written by the son and grandson of the tomb owner, who followed in the footsteps of Djehutynakht. If this is correct, Djehutynakht must already have been an old man when the graffito was written (in year 13) of nomarch Ahanakht I. This implication suggests that his career must have started well before the rule of the nomarch, and thus still during the First Intermediate Period.

Support for this conclusion is found in the execution of the restoration inscriptions carved by the nomarch Djehutynakht, son of Teti, in two Old Kingdom rock tombs in the cemetery on the south side of the Wadi Deir en-Nakhleh and in another on the north slope.[108] The execution of the texts is strikingly similar to that of the inscriptions in Tombs 102 and 104 (including, e.g., the characteristic use of red guidelines discussed above by van Walsem). As Brovarski has argued, the nomarch in whose days the restoration inscriptions were written down was probably the predecessor of Ahanakht I.[109]

Although the inscription in Tomb 104 itself probably dates from the post-unification 11th Dynasty, its contents may reflect organizational aspects of the provincial government of the late Heracleopolitan Period.[110]

108. For the graffiti, which were rediscovered by the Joint Expedition, see Brovarski, "Ahanakht of Bersheh," in *Studies in Anc. Eg.*, p. 22, note 27 (with literature).

109. Ibid., p. 22, note 31.

110. Ibid., pp. 26–30 for arguments suggesting a different date.

CHAPTER IV

ART HISTORICAL OVERVIEW

Rita E. Freed

A. Introduction

The Middle Kingdom reliefs of Middle Egypt are, for the most part, published in line drawing, incompletely, or not at all. In an attempt to shed light on the internal development of this material and the interrelations among the different sites, an art historical analysis of the tomb decoration was included as a component of the Joint Boston-Pennsylvania and Leiden Expedition to Bersheh. In the course of the 1990 season, both the Old Kingdom and Middle Kingdom tombs were surveyed, and an analysis, primarily of the 11th Dynasty material, was undertaken. Preliminary results reveal that, while details of style and iconography of each tomb may be specific to a given tomb, general trends unique to Bersheh and to the region are present. Below is a brief discussion of selected aspects of the relief style and iconography of the tombs of Ahanakht I, Djehutynakht VI, Iha, Nehri I and Nehri II, and an overview of common aspects in the art of Bersheh.

B. Tomb 5 – The Tomb of Ahanakht

The two-chambered tomb of Ahanakht is one of the largest and best preserved of the decorated Middle Kingdom tombs at Bersheh. Its decoration, as in all the other tombs discussed below, was executed in sunk relief on a thinly plastered limestone surface. While in many areas the plaster has been lost, and along with it painted details and delicate interior modeling, the decoration was so deeply carved that outlines often remain in the limestone bedrock. One of the most striking aspects of Ahanakht's tomb is that the inner and outer chamber display different styles of figural modeling, undoubtedly reflecting different hands. This feature is especially clear in minor vignettes. In the inner chamber, elongated figures with high, narrow waists, short upper bodies and small heads (fig. 40) resemble what appears particularly in Upper Egypt prior to the reunification by Mentuhotep II (fig. 41).[111]

In addition, a number of the vignettes chosen and the manner in which they are rendered likewise reflect contact with or knowledge of Upper Egyptian pre-reunification style and iconography. For example, on the eastern half of the south wall are two milking scenes where one man holds the rear legs of a cow, as another man kneeling with one knee up and balancing a narrow-necked jar on the upraised knee, milks her (fig. 42). This is the same manner in which the scene is rendered in the tombs and on the sarcophagi of Mentuhotep II's minor queens (fig. 43). The milking scene is, to be sure, Old Kingdom in derivation, but Old Kingdom examples (fig. 44) tend to show the rear legs of the cow tied together and the vessel into which the milk flows placed on the ground.[112] Another example of an Upper Egyptian vignette associated with pre-reunification times is the image of jousting bulls (fig. 45) which appears three times in the innermost chamber of Ahanakht's tomb. This motif is found from late Dynasty 6 on from Deshasha to Aswan,[113] but it never appears at Giza or Saqqara.[114]

In contrast, the outer chamber presents a different picture in terms of style and iconography. Many of its themes, which include bird-trapping, fishing, cattle fording a river (fig. 46), bull sacrifice, cattle in procession, the dragging of a stubborn donkey, and dancing figures are straight from the genre scene repertory of the Old Kingdom. Moreover, they are executed with a staid, studied deliberateness, as if they were copied. Unlike what is seen on minor figures in the inner chamber, the proportions of the minor figures in the outer chamber are consistent with the Old Kingdom canon (compare fig. 40 and fig. 46).

Because the large-scale figures, seated and standing, in both chambers are virtually identical in terms of canon, position, costume, and attributes, it seems likely that the same artisan carved or at least

111. The differences between the First Intermediate Period and Middle Kingdom canons are articulated by H. Ranke, "Beiträge zum Kanonproblem" *ZÄS* 84 (1959), pp. 113–119.

112. L. Klebs, *Die Reliefs und Malereien des mittleren Reiches*, p. 90, n. 1, first noted the differences between the Old Kingdom and Middle Kingdom milking scenes.

113. Representative examples are as follows: Deshasheh, the tomb of Shedu, in W. M. F. Petrie, *Deshasheh*, pl. XVIII; Meir, the tomb of Pepy-ankh (A, No. 2), in A. M. Blackman and M. R. Apted, *The Rock Tombs of Meir* V, pl. 32; Hawawish, the tomb of Kheni, in N. Kanawati, *The Rock Tombs of El-Hawawish, The Cemetery of Akhmim* II, fig. 20; and Thebes, the tomb of *ꜣInỉ-ỉtỉ⸗f*, in B. Jaroš-Deckert, Grabung im Asasif 1963–1970. Band V. *Das Grab des ꜣInỉ-ỉtỉ.f, Die Wandmalereien der XI Dynastie*, pl. 18. In *ꜣInỉ-ỉtỉ⸗f*'s tomb, the jousting bulls are located on Pillar II, face C, the painting of which the author attributes to a local Theban atelier. For elucidation of contributions of each painting school, see ibid., pl. 12. For further discussion of the styles represented in the tomb and their implications for dating, see below, note 115.

114. Y. Harpur, *Decoration in Egyptian Tombs of the Old Kingdom*, p. 11, n. 12, cites the image of fighting bulls as one of the few examples where it is valid to speak of a motif that is exclusively Upper Egyptian in style.

Fig. 40. Attendants from the inner chamber of the tomb of Ahanakht (Tomb 5), exhibiting the pre-reunification canon.

Fig. 41. Offering bearers from the sarcophagus of Ashait from Deir el-Bahari (Cairo JE 47267), reign of Mentuhotep II, exhibiting the pre-reunification canon.

Fig. 42. Milking scene from the inner chamber of the tomb of Ahanakht.

Fig. 43. Milking scene from the sarcophagus of Kawit from Deir el-Bahari (Cairo JE 47397), reign of Mentuhotep II, pre-reunification style.

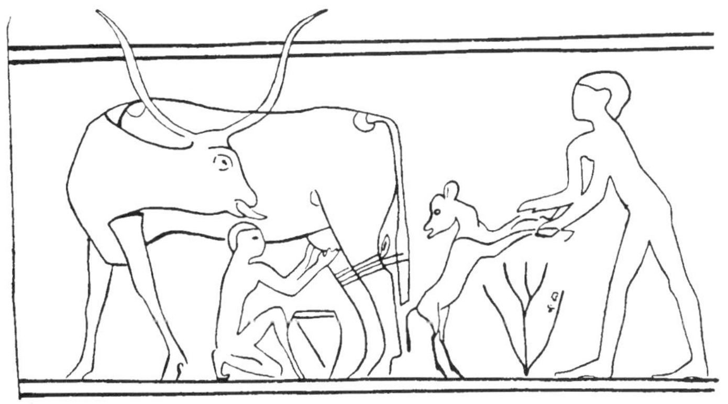

Fig. 44. Milking scene from the tomb of Akh-meret-nisut at Giza, G 2184, Dynasty 5.

Fig. 45. Jousting bulls from the inner chamber of the tomb of Ahanakht.

Fig. 46. Boatmen assisting cattle across the river, from the outer chamber of the tomb of Ahanakht.

laid out the large scale figures in both, probably as one of the first stages in the decoration of the tomb. As with the minor figures, proportionally the large figures too (fig. 47) are correct according to the Old Kingdom canon (fig. 48).

From this evidence, the following conclusions are suggested: At least two artisans (or two groups) worked on the tomb of Ahanakht. A "master" influenced by the North executed the scenes in the outer chamber and the large scale figures in both. A second, who worked exclusively in the inner chamber, was trained in the Theban school before the reunification.[115] In terms of dating, it seems likely that the tomb is a product of the period immediately following the reunification, that is, late in the reign of Mentuhotep II. At that time there is a burst of building activity throughout the country and presumably also a resurgence of "national consciousness," a phenomenon which might explain the appearance of such "national symbols" as the heraldic plants of Upper and Lower Egypt, specifically the lotus and papyrus, which appear as incised columns on the side edges of the south and north chambers respectively. Where they are fully preserved, the columns rise to the full height of the walls and define the boundaries of the room. A dating just after the reunification for the tomb of Ahanakht places it at the early end of the date proposed by Willems[116] and immediately following the date suggested by Brovarski.[117]

One additional point may be noted in the context of this discussion of Ahanakht's tomb. The delicate feathering of the ducks found on the south wall of the outer chamber (fig. 49) and the skillful blending of their pastel tones betray the hand of a master. Because the treatment of the geese on the famous "Bersheh coffin"[118] (fig. 50) belonging to a

115. A comparative situation was noted by Jaroš-Deckert in the tomb of *ʾInỉ-ỉtỉ⸗f* at Thebes (*Grab… ʾInỉ-ỉtỉ.f*, pp. 127–28), where she identified a local Theban painting style, a canonical painting style, and a style that is intermediate between the two. The author dates this tomb prior to the reunification on the basis of the spelling of the king's prenomen on one of the pillars (pp. 63, 117–19). H. Willems in "Review of B. Jaroš-Deckert, Grabung im Asasif 1963–1970. Band 5: *Das Grab des ʾInỉ-ỉtỉ.f*," *BiOr* 46 (1989), cols. 598–599, notes that while the decoration of this tomb certainly began before the reunification, it is possible that parts were executed after the reunification, based on the canonical art style in some areas and the nature of the battles represented.

116. Harco Willlems dates the tomb of Ahanakht to "the last three decades of the XIth Dynasty" in "The Nomarchs of the Hare Nome and Early Middle Kingdom History," *JEOL* 28 (1983–84), p. 102, n. 153.

117. Brovarski, "Ahanakht of Bersheh," in *Studies in Anc. Eg.*, p. 29.

118. See Terrace, *Egyptian Paintings*, for a depiction of this coffin now in the Museum of Fine Arts, Boston (MFA 20.1822).

Fig. 47. Large-scale figure of Ahanakht on the east side of the doorway between the chambers in Tomb 5.

Fig. 48. Large-scale figure of Kaemnofret from his tomb at Saqqara, Dynasty 5; MFA 04.1761.

Fig. 49. Geese from the south wall of outer chamber of the tomb of Ahanakht showing delicate feathering.

Fig. 50. Geese from the coffin of Djehutynakht IV (Tomb 10), showing delicate feathering.

man named Djehutynakht is so similar, it is quite possible that the same artisan worked on both, probably within a fairly short time span. This would suggest that the Djehutynakht in question is to be identified as Djehutynakht IV, son of Ahanakht.[119]

C. Tombs 102 and 104 – The Tombs of Iha and Djehutynakht

Two subordinates of the nomarch Ahanakht (Tombs 102 and 104) are located on the cliff face directly under that of their patron and are separated by a third undecorated tomb (Tomb 103). Similar in size, orientation and iconography, they were probably executed at the same time and by the same workshop. Close comparison, however, reveals subtle differences, perhaps explainable as varying workmanship of different artisans.[120]

The tombs are small, single-chambered structures whose floors are all but completely taken up by burial shafts. Both share an object frieze on the south wall consisting of provisions on long, low tables which are suspended well above their baselines. (Djehutynakht's tomb continues the frieze on the north wall as well.) Additionally, both display a narrow false door with a thick frame on the west wall and, on the east wall, piled offerings on the south end followed by menu lists containing stick-like figures of kneeling offering bearers and, below, a register of slender herdsman dwarfed by the muscular, massive cows they lead.

The tombs differ significantly in the degree of regularity of layout and design. Red grid lines are omnipresent in Iha's tomb in the horizontal and vertical spacing of the inscription, in individual hieroglyphs (fig. 51) and in the broad layout of the figural register.[121] As a result there is an overall regularity to the inscription. This feature is also manifest in the piled offerings on the east wall, which display a balanced, bilateral symmetry in

Fig. 51. Inscription from the tomb of Iha (Tomb 102), showing horizontal and vertical guidelines.

their layout. In contrast, in Djehutynakht's tomb, there are only occasional traces of gridlines defining the upper and lower borders of the inscription, and very rarely are they present for either individual signs or figural registers. Predictably, hieroglyphs are often inconsistent, tilted, or uneven, and offerings are sometimes askew (fig. 52). The regularly spaced cattle procession on the bottom register of the south wall in Iha's tomb dissolves in Djehutynakht's into a hunting scene. Accordingly, in the middle of the procession, without transition and without additional baselines, an oryx hovers above a placid cow, while behind the cow a hound attacks another oryx. By emphasizing the salient aspects of each animal, namely the brawny bodies of the cattle, the fragile limbs of the oryx, and the sinewy torso of the hound, the artisan has conveyed a vitality missing from the more rigidly laid out tomb of Iha. In all likelihood, it was executed by a different hand but one that followed a similar model.

Both tombs are probably contemporary with each other and approximately contemporary with the tomb of their master, Ahanakht, based on their similarity of subject matter, layout, and carving technique.[122] Figural proportions conforming to

119. Brovarski, "Ahanakht of Bersheh," in *Studies in Anc. Eg.*, pp. 25 and 29, and Willems, *Chests of Life*, pp. 70–71, both identify him as either Djehutynakht IV (son of Ahanakht) or Djehutynakht V (son of Nehri I), who lived somewhat later.

120. Van Walsem and Willems agree that the same workshop executed both tombs, and Willems notes additionally their similar "paleographic peculiarities" (p. 48 in this volume). Both scholars are inclined, however, to see the same artists at work in both tombs (p. 48), a point on which we differ.

121. In no instance, however, do canonical grid lines presently mark out parts of the figures.

122. In addition, Ahanakht is mentioned repeatedly in the tombs of both of his subordinates. See *El Bersheh* II, pp. 38–41, 43–46.

Fig. 52. Inscription from the tomb of Djehutynakht (Tomb 104) showing skewed hieroglyphs.

the Old Kingdom canon support a date after the reunification for these two tombs as well.

D. Tomb 19 – The Tomb of Nehri I

Of the decoration of this two-chambered tomb of the nomarch Nehri I (Tomb 19), only a few blocks remain in situ and several others lie scattered in the vicinity. However, the chance discovery in the 1990 season, on the cliff face just south of the tomb, of a block which fits directly atop the west side of the outer chamber's north wall (fig. 31) offers the hope that additional blocks will appear when a systematic search is conducted.

The decoration displays a fascinating combination of material. The agricultural scenes, including such themes as hoeing, the driving of cattle, and the ensnaring of birds in a clapnet found on the large blocks lying just south of the tomb,[123] represent some of the most traditional of the Old Kingdom repertoire. In contrast, the pretzel-like contortions of the wrestlers visible on a block photographed by Reisner in 1915 (fig. 53) but no longer preserved, appear to be similar to those from Middle Kingdom Beni Hasan and Meir.[124] They resemble in particular the larger, more full-bodied forms from the tomb of Senbi at the latter site, which is attributed to the reign of Amenemhat I.[125] A griffin, monkeys, and baboons on a Bersheh fragment illustrated by Newberry[126] offer additional examples of unusual iconography shared by Bersheh and Beni Hasan.[127]

In manner of representation as well, Nehri's tomb displays some strong affinities to nearby contemporary sites. For example, generally a large-scale female figure stands with both feet together. Nehri's wife, however, stands behind Nehri on the west half of the rear wall of the outer chamber with her feet apart so that the toe of her forward foot is visible under the arch of his rear foot. As if to emphasize this wide stance, the artisan has indicated the full line of her legs underneath her tight-fitting garment. Although aspects of this manner of rendering the female form[128] are found elsewhere in Middle Egypt, nowhere is it as closely paralleled as at Meir in the tomb of Ukhotep, son of Senbi,[129] attributed by the excavator to the reign of Sesostris I on the basis of genealogical information.[130] Another unusual detail is the manner in which Nehri I carries the lotus flower, specifically, in his rear hand and facing to the rear. This gesture is also found in Ukhotep's tomb.[131]

It seems clear from the iconographic evidence that the artisans who worked on Nehri I's tomb had contact with art or artisans from nearby centers. While the subjects shown and the manner in which they are represented bears the greatest similarity to the early 12th Dynasty tombs at Meir, the style of carving, exemplified by a deep outline and a broad cut angled in sharply to meet it, is similar to what is found at Assiut in the tomb of Khety II, dated by cartouche to the reign of Merikare.[132] In both instances a layer of plaster would have obliterated the angularity of the carving.

Nehri I, who figures prominently in the Hatnub graffiti,[133] has been dated as early as the end of the Herakleopolitan Period[134] and as late as Dynasty 12.[135] The latest regnal year date found in association with him is eight.[136] Unfortunately, the

123. Presumably they are from the outer chamber and were thrust forward when the tomb collapsed; see above, p. 30 and fig. 30. For a possible explanation of the destruction, see Willems, "Deir El-Bersheh," *GM* 110 (1989), p. 76.

124. Beni Hasan: P. E. Newberry, *Beni Hasan* I, pls. XIV–XVI, and *Beni Hasan* II, pls. V, XV and XXII; Meir: A. M. Blackman, *The Rock Tombs of Meir* I, pl. III.

125. Blackman, *The Rock Tombs of Meir* I, pp. 8 and 11. Willems narrows the dating to the second half of the reign, see *Chests of Life*, p. 84.

126. *El Bersheh* II, Plate XI, No. 5. Unfortunately, this block was not found during the 1990 season.

127. For a detailed discussion of the similarities between the tombs of Ahanakht and Nehri I at Bersheh, and Baket and Khety at Beni Hasan, see Brovarski, "Ahanakht of Bersheh," in *Studies in Anc. Eg.*, p. 28. For another discussion of the dating of the tombs at both sites, see D. Spanel, "Toward a Reassessment of the Herakleopolitan Period and the Eleventh Dynasty: The Date of the Djehutynakht-Family Coffins from Bersheh (B1Bo–B7Bo)," forthcoming. I am grateful to Dr. Spanel for sharing this information with me.

128. This discussion refers to females depicted on a large scale, presumably main family members, rather than female attendants or offering bearers, for whom this pose is more common.

129. Blackman, *The Rock Tombs of Meir* II, pl. XIII.

130. Blackman, *The Rock Tombs of Meir* I, p. 8 and *The Rock Tombs of Meir* II, p. 11, where it is noted that the tomb of his "great nephew" contains the cartouches of Amenemhat II.

131. Blackman, *The Rock Tombs of Meir* II, pl. V.

132. Spanel, however, suggests that "although Khety II obviously was Merikare's contemporary, the tomb itself may postdate the king's reign, perhaps belonging to the re-unification;" see "Reassessment of the Herakleopolitan Period."

133. *Hatnub*, pp. 32–66, Graffiti nos. 14–29.

134. *Hatnub*, p. 93.

135. W. Schenkel, *Frühmittelägyptische Studien*, §§ 94–95. For a recent overview of opinions on the dating of Nehri I, see Willems, "Nomarchs of the Hare Nome," *JEOL* 28 (1983–84), pp. 80-102.

Fig. 53. Wrestlers from the tomb of Nehri I (Tomb 19).

closest parallels in terms of style and iconography are themselves not well dated. More work is needed in this area before conclusions can be drawn. Hopefully, the work of the Boston-Penn-Leiden Expedition will shed more light on some of these issues.

E. Tomb 1 – The Tomb of Nehri II

Little can be said about this tomb stylistically, since the plaster into which the wall decoration was carved has fallen away.[137] Perhaps the plaster was thicker here or the relief not as deeply incised. Almost nothing is visible in the smoothed limestone bedrock of the walls.[138] Only careful observation under various lighting conditions by the University of Pennsylvania team revealed faint traces of carving. Remains of a menu list with kneeling figures of offering bearers, a large pile of offerings including *bꜣḳ* plants,[139] and a false door on the west wall, are consistent with what is found in the post-reunification tombs of Ahanakht and his subordinates. However, the large-scale figures of the owner and his wife on the west wall facing

136. Anthes, *Hatnub*, pp. 59–65, Graffiti Nr. 26–28.

137. In most of the tombs discussed above, the plaster is gone but the decoration is visible underneath.

138. For the Coffin Texts which still cover the ceiling, see the discussion of Nehri II's tomb by David Silverman, pp. 15–27 in this volume.

toward the entrance and a similarly large scale figure on the east wall are more comparable to what is found in the tomb of Nehri II's son Djehutynakht VI (No. 21, to be more closely examined in a future season). Nehri II's other son, Amenemhat, was in office, according to Hatnub Graffito no. 49,[140] in year 31 of Sesostris I. Once the walls are cleaned completely, the hope is that additional iconographic evidence will appear.[141] At that time perhaps it will be possible to determine a more specific date for the tomb.

F. Conclusions

From this art historical overview of the tombs examined during the 1990 season at Bersheh, several preliminary observations may be made. First, travel by and contacts among the artisans who decorated the 11th Dynasty tombs was perhaps more widespread than generally realized. The most straightforward explanation for the pre-unification Theban area style and iconography in the post-reunification tomb of Ahanakht is that Theban-trained artisans worked on it, probably side-by-side with artisans from the North. Another possibility is that the post-reunification style really existed in the North throughout the Heracleopolitan Period on a much broader scale and in a much larger geographical area than previously assumed.[142] One might then postulate that both artisans/schools worked side by side prior to the completion of the reunification just as they may have done in the tomb of the general Intef at Thebes.[143]

Although the later tombs do not readily reveal such far-flung influences, perhaps because of the greater tendency toward a more unified style country-wide by the end of Dynasty 11, there is no doubt that regionally a common artistic milieu existed. This suggestion best accounts for such unusual iconography as the wrestlers, griffins, and baboons, for example, which the Bersheh tombs share with Beni Hasan and Meir, or the unusual stance and attributes Nehri and his wife have in common with Ukhotep and his wife at Meir. Future investigations of these sites may even show that some of the same artisans worked at many of them, traveling from commission to commission.

Even within the common artistic milieu, local custom and tradition played a role as well. For example, the menu list accompanied by fairly large kneeling figures of offering bearers, the shape and manner of carving the false door, and one or more *bꜣḳ* plants (moringa)[144] among the offerings appear in the majority of tombs discussed above, even when their owners are unrelated.

In most of the tombs examined, the animals are rendered naturalistically and masterfully.[145] For humans, on the other hand, the artisans appear to have been consistently much less confident, so that even within the same tomb, stick-figure-like caricatures share the same register with their more full bodied, but often awkward, counterparts. Perhaps this general lack of consistency in the rendering of the human form is a consequence of the newly altered canon and the artificial constraints placed upon artisans as a result.

These conclusions are offered as working hypotheses to be tested in future seasons, when the Boston-Pennsylvania-Leiden expedition hopes to continue and broaden its examination of the tombs both at Bersheh and throughout the region.

139. The *bꜣḳ* has been identified as moringa, a small tree with whip-like branches indigenous to Egypt. From the nut, a sweet oil is extracted. Used in cosmetics, perfumes, and medicines, its value lies, at least in part, in the fact that it does not become rancid. The *bꜣḳ* is associated with Thoth, the area's local god. For information and bibliography on the *bꜣḳ* see R. Germer, "Moringaölbaum," *LÄ* IV (1983), cols. 206–207.

140. *Hatnub*, pp. 76–77.

141. For the genealogical evidence, see especially Willems, "Nomarchs of the Hare Nome," *JEOL* 28 (1983–1984), pp. 83–84 and idem, *Chests of Life*, p. 71, genealogical chart.

142. Spanel alludes to this possibility in "Reassessment of the Heracleopolitan Period," forthcoming.

143. For the dating of this tomb, see above, notes 113 and 115.

144. See n. 139 for information on *bꜣḳ* plants.

145. The exception is the tomb of Nehri II, where neither animals nor humans are sufficiently well preserved to permit any conclusions.

CHAPTER V

OTHER WORK

Edward Brovarski

Melissa Robinson

Jean-Louis Lachevre

A. Site Reconaissance

1. *Lower Terrace: The Decree of King Neferefre*

The Expedition staff located and photographed the short decree or letter of King Neferefre (Horus *Nfr-ḫʿw*) on the facade of Fraser's Tomb D (c) on a narrow platform some distance below the high terrace (fig. 54).[146] The decree is addressed to the Count and Controller of the Two Thrones, *Ỉʿ-ỉb*. Anthes' copy appears to be correct, but in a future season the expedition plans to make a collation and compare it to the earlier version. At that time it may be possible to add a few more signs.

Fig. 54. Facade D (c) with 5th Dynasty decree of King Neferefre.

2. *South Side of the Wadi*

Fraser counted seventy-two tombs and a large number of shafts on the south side of the Wadi Deir en-Nakhleh. According to him only four of these had any inscriptions. During the 1990 season the expedition was able to identify and make hand copies of the texts in two of the tombs.

The Tomb of Ankhy

Fraser's Tomb Q (b) is divided in two by an architrave that extends east to west across its width.[147] The architrave is inscribed and reads: "An offering which the king gives and Anubis, Who-presides-over-the-divine-booth, that he be buried in the necropolis, after he has become very old, as one honored by the great god, and that offerings be invoked for him on the New Year's Day festival, the festival of Thoth... the *Wꜣg*-festival, the procession of Sokar, and the festival of the Great Burning, (namely) the estate manager, sole friend, lector priest, and chamberlain, one honored by Ptah and by He-who-is-in-Khemenu, Ankhy."

The inner part of the tomb in particular is irregular and unfinished, but the outer chamber preserves its original wall decoration to a considerable extent, all executed in a flat, sharp-edged, raised relief (fig. 55). Only the entrance wall is undecorated. A false door dedicated to Ankhy occupies a position on the right-hand (west) wall towards the front. To the left of the false door, Ankhy stands, facing out toward his eldest son, "the sole friend, lector priest, and scribe of the divine book, Mery-ib." A short column squeezed in behind Ankhy reads: "His son whom he loves, Khnumu." Further to the left Ankhy (now effaced) is seated before a low, rectangular table bearing loaves of bread. At a later date, when the tomb of Ankhy was presumably used as a dwelling, a large opening was cut through the offering table into an adjacent tomb (fig. 56).

The left-hand (east) wall is occupied by a large table scene. Ankhy sits behind a pedestal table surmounted by tall, conventionalized slices of bread. Before him stand two men offering birds and a third man with a haunch. Other offering-bearers follow. As on the opposite wall, Ankhy's figure is damaged, while a large opening has been cut out above his head that opens into a neighboring tomb on the east. In the inscriptions accompanying all three scenes, Ankhy is *ỉmꜣḫw ḫr Ḏḥwty ỉmy Ḫmnw*, "honored by Thoth Who-is-in-Khemenu."

The architrave that bisects the tomb into unequal parts is supported by two stone columns in which statues were cut in the round. The column on the left (eastern side) has a standing male figure in a flaring wig, now much defaced. The statue on the right (western) column was never completed.

In the right-hand (western) thickness between the front and back portions of the tomb is a panel showing Ankhy embraced by his wife Nebkau/Iwenus (*Nb-kꜣw rn⸗s nfr Iwn[w?]⸗s*). The figures face outward.

146. *El Bersheh* II, pp. 56–57, and Hatnub, Graffito no. 15.

147. Cf. *El Bersheh* II, p.64 and Cledat, "Notes sur la nécropole de Bersheh," *BIFAO* 1 (1901), pp. 101–2.

Fig. 55. The west wall of the tomb of Ankhy, Tomb Q (b), with false door and "window" cut through the offering scene.

Fig. 56. Portion of effaced figure of Ankhy and accompanying inscriptions from the west wall of Tomb Q (b).

Fig. 57. Doorway to shrine in the tomb of Impy, Tomb S (x). The restoration decree of the nomarch Djehutynakht, born of Teti, is to the lower right of the door.

Sunk in the floor of the outer chamber are two square pits and a sloping shaft. The pits stand open and lead to burial chambers; the shaft is filled with debris. In the back wall of the inner chamber, there is in addition a sloping shaft once closed with a stone slab similar to that in the tomb of Nehri II (No. 1).

The Tomb of Impy

On a slightly lower level than that of the tomb of Ankhy is a sepulcher on a larger scale than many of the others on this side of the wadi. Fraser's Tomb S (x) has a plain facade and central doorway with an uninscribed lintel above leading into a rectangular chamber (fig. 57).[148] In the center of its rear wall is a doorway into a small unfinished shrine. The doorposts and jambs of this doorway are inscribed with the name and titles of the tomb owner, the *mḏḥ zšw nswt… ḥkꜣ ḥwt ḥry-tp nswt pr-ꜥꜣ ꜣImpy*, "overseer of royal scribes,… estate manager, and chamberlain of the palace, Impy." In the wall of the main chamber on either side of the door are niches with remains of badly damaged seated figures cut in them. On the rear wall to the right of the door is one of the two restoration inscriptions of Djehutynakht, born of Teti, referred to above (p. 50).

148. Cf. *El Bersheh* II, pp. 64–65 and Cledat, "Notes sur la nécropole de Bersheh," p. 102.

B. The Bersheh Mapping Project

In 1988 and 1989, members of the Expedition staff conducted brief feasibility studies for an epigraphic survey, including a walking survey of the tombs on the northern side of the wadi and the quarries.[149] There they rediscovered many unmapped rock-cut tombs on the northern side, found numerous inscriptions and architectural remains in the quarries, and located mud-brick architecture partially buried by the sand on the low desert to the west. In 1990 the Dutch and American teams returned to the site for a preliminary epigraphic season, during which

149. Willems, "Deir el-Bersheh," *GM* 110 (1989), pp. 75–95.

they also carried out a walking survey of the south side of the wadi. This latter survey confirmed the presence of many rock-cut tombs and shafts noted in Blackden and Fraser's descriptions of the area.

During future seasons, the expedition plans to map the Wadi Deir en-Nakhleh, the hillsides to the north and south, and the low desert to the west. The project will generate maps at the scales of 1 centimeter to 500 centimeters (1:500), 1:250, 1:100, and 1:50. Separate plans and sections for archaeologically or architecturally significant squares will be made by the archaeologist or architect at the scales of 1:100, 1:50, and 1:10.

The first step in mapping the necropolis will be the establishment of datum (or control) points, and the determination of the orientation of these points with regard to true north by means of astronomical observation. One datum will be selected as the principal or alpha point, and the elevation of this point as well as the elevations of the other control points will be determined with relation to sea level.

Next, the surveying team will construct a control grid originating at the principal datum point. This grid will divide the site into 25 x 25 meter squares which, in turn, will be sub-divided into 5 x 5 meter squares.

One of the goals of the mapping project is the production of a topographic map of the Bersheh necropolis with a contour interval of 1.0 meter. Ultimately the site grid will be placed as an overlay upon the topographic map and will provide the basis for the mapping of archaeological and architectural features.

C. The Bersheh Object Database

One of the major goals of the Bersheh Project is the construction of a computerized relational database of the various objects originating from the necropolis that are now in the private and public collections around the world. It will also include any objects or loose blocks found during clearing, routine excavation or sampling. In the case of these latter objects, it will be possible to enter a precise survey grid location. Information for the database will be gathered from the *Topographical Bibliography* compiled by Porter and Moss, from site and museum publications, field diaries, and museum correspondence. The expedition is in the process of developing a format to provide as much information as possible utilizing "fields" as various as *material, publication, field no., tomb/shaft no.*, etc. The database fields *memo* (for lengthy text) and *graphics* (for scanned images) will also be used to make the database record as comprehensive as possible. Unfortunately, it will not be possible to utilize all fields for every object stored in the database due to deficiencies in early records from the site, but every attempt will be made to obtain as much information about each object as possible. Additional databases will be created that will include transcriptions and translations of inscriptions, titles, paleographic and iconographic details, drawings, illustrations, etc. Each of these subsidiary databases will be linked to the "master" database. Suggestions for improvements to our database structure, information on additional objects and existing databases for specialized purposes are welcome.

D. Conservation Report

The expedition conservator was responsible for evaluating the physical stability and present condition of the remains of four tombs, for helping to develop an approach for examining and documenting each site, for assisting in determining future conservation policies, priorities, and storage requirements, and for helping to develop plans for the clearance of Tomb 21.

Before work could begin, it was necessary to establish safety measures for the protection of the staff. Each tomb was examined for structural stability. Tomb 103 proved to be structurally secure. Tombs 1 and 5 were determined to be stable enough to allow epigraphic activities, but neither would withstand violent natural or mechanical vibration. Tomb 21, however, presented hazardous work conditions due to the precarious position of the stone slabs and the amount of debris near the shafts inside the tomb. Tombs 1, 5, and 102 each contain deep burial shafts rimmed by narrow ledges. These shafts were covered each day with sheets of reinforced plywood to permit safe access to the chamber walls and ceilings. The staff was required to work in groups of twos and threes and to wear harnesses both on the surrounding hillside and during exploration of unstable areas within certain tombs.

The appropriate expedition staff member and the conservator surveyed each tomb to determine the extent of archaeological remains, and the conservator systematically documented the condition of all extant wall and ceiling decorations by written report and photograph. Superficial cleaning of surface dust and mud was necessary in Tombs 1 and 5 in order to allow the epigraphers to record scenes and inscriptions accurately. These minimal cleaning procedures proved to be most valuable to the initial examination of these tombs. This preliminary survey, however, revealed the need for additional cleaning to allow the recording of all decorated chambers and loose blocks.

As most of the south and part of the east walls as well as one-third of the ceiling of Tomb 1 are now missing, the decoration on the remaining walls is fully exposed to the elements and to visitors. The conservator prepared plans, at the request of the Egyptian Antiquities Organization, for permanent enclosure of the tomb using a stone wall, tin roof, and steel gate.

BIBLIOGRAPHY

Anthes, Rudolf.
Die Felseninschriften von Hatnub. UGAÄ 9. Leipzig: J.C. Hinrichs, 1928.

Barta, Winfried.
Aufbau und Bedeutung der altägyptischen Opferformel. AF 24. Glückstadt-Hamburg: J.J. Augustin, 1968.

Blackman, A.M.
The Rock Tombs of Meir I. ASE 22. London: Egypt Exploration Fund, 1914.

Blackman, A.M. and Apted, M.R.
The Rock Tombs of Meir V. ASE 28. London: Egypt Exploration Society, 1953.

Brovarski, Edward.
Canopics. Corpus Antiquitatum Aegyptiacarum, Museum of Fine Arts, Boston, fasc. 1. Mainz am Rhein: Philipp von Zabern, 1978.

————
"Ahanakht of Bersheh and the Hare Nome in the First Intermediate Period and Middle Kingdom," pp. 14–30. In *Studies in Ancient Egypt, the Aegean, and the Sudan: Essays in Honor of Dows Dunham on the occasion of his 90th birthday, June 1, 1980.* Edited by William K. Simpson and Whitney M. Davis. Boston: Museum of Fine Arts, 1981.

————, editor.
A Table of Offerings: 17 Years of Acquisitions of Egyptian and Ancient Near Eastern Art by William Kelly Simpson for the Museum of Fine Arts. Boston: Museum of Fine Arts, 1987.

de Buck, Adriaan.
The Egyptian Coffin Texts VII. Oriental Institute Publications, Vol. 87. Chicago: The University of Chicago Press, 1961.

Cledat, Jean.
"Notes sur la nécropole de Bersheh." *BIFAO* 1 (1901), pp. 101–102.

Daressy, Georges.
"Fouilles de Deir el Bircheh (Novembre-Décembre 1897)." *ASAE* 1 (1900): 22–43.

D'Auria, Sue, Lacovara, Peter and Roehrig, Catharine H.
Mummies and Magic: The Funerary Arts of Ancient Egypt. Boston: Museum of Fine Arts, 1988.

Dunham, Dows.
"The Tomb of Dehuti-nekht and His Wife, about 2000 B.C." *BMFA* 19 (1921), pp. 43–46.

Dunham, Dows and Smith, William Stevenson.
"A Middle Kingdom Painted Coffin from Deir el Bersheh," pp. 261–68. In *Studi in Memoria di Ippolito Rosellini nel primo centenario della Morte.* Vol. 1. Pisa: Industrie Grafiche V. Lischi E. Figli, 1949.

Fecht, G.
Wortakzent und Silbenstruktur. AF 21. Glückstadt: J.J. Augustin, 1960.

Fischer, H. G.
"Redundant Determinatives in the Old Kingdom." *MMJ* 8 (1973), pp. 7–25.

Germer, R.
"Moringaölbaum," cols. 206–207. In *Lexikon der Ägyptologie* IV. Edited by Wolfgang Helck and Eberhard Otto. Wiesbaden: Otto Harrassowitz, 1983.

Griffith, F.Ll. and Newberry, P.E.
El Bersheh II. ASE 4. London: Egypt Exploration Fund, 1894.

Harpur, Yvonne.
Decoration in Egyptian Tombs of the Old Kingdom. London and New York: Kegan Paul International, 1987.

Harvard University–Museum of Fine Arts, Boston, Bersheh Expedition.
Bersheh Diary, 1915 (unpublished).

Houlihan, Patrick F.
The Birds of Ancient Egypt. Cairo: American University in Cairo Press, 1986.

Jaroš-Deckert, B.
Das Grab des Ỉnỉ-ỉtỉ.f, Die Wandmalereien der XI. Dynastie. Grabung im Asasif 1963–1970. Band V. Mainz am Rhein: Philipp von Zabern, 1984.

Kamal, Ahmed Bey
"Fouilles à Déïr-el-Barsheh (mars-avril 1900)." *ASAE* 2 (1901), pp. 14–43.

———
"Fouilles à Deir-el-Barché exécutées dans les six premiers mois de l'année par M. Antonini de Mallawi." *ASAE* 3 (1902), pp. 276–82.

———
"Rapport sur les fouilles exécutées à Deïr el-Barshé en janvier, février, mars 1901." *ASAE* 2 (1901), pp. 206–22.

Kanawati, N.
The Rock Tombs of El-Hawawish, The Cemetery of Akhmim II. Sydney: Macquarie Ancient History Association, 1981.

Kemp, B.J.
Ancient Egypt, Anatomy of a Civilization. London and New York: Routledge, 1989.

Klebs, L.
Die Reliefs und Malereien des mittleren Reiches. Heidelberg: C. Winter, 1922.

Leclant, J.
"Fouilles et travaux en Egypte et au Soudan, 1969–1970." *Or* 40 (1971), p. 234.

———
"Fouilles et travaux en Egypte et au Soudan, 1971–1972." *Or* 42 (1973), p. 405.

Lesko, Leonard H.
The Ancient Egyptian Book of Two Ways. University of California Publications, Near Eastern Studies, Vol. 17. Berkeley: University of California Press, 1972.

Newberry, Percy E.
Beni Hasan I and II. ASE 1 and 2. London: Egypt Exploration Fund, 1893–1894.

———
El Bersheh I: *The Tomb of Tehutihetep.* ASE 3. London: Egypt Exploration Fund, 1893.

Petrie, W.M.F.
Deshasheh. 15th Memoir of the Egypt Exploration Fund. London: Egypt Exploration Fund, 1898.

Petrie, W.M.F.
Tools and Weapons. BSEA 30. London: Bernard Quaritch, 1917.

Posener-Kriéger, Paule
Les archives du temple funeraire de Néferirkarê-kakaï (Les Papyrus d'Abousir). Cairo: Institut Français d'Archéologie Orientale, 1976.

Ranke, H.
"Beiträge zum Kanonproblem." *ZÄS* 84 (1959), pp. 113–119.

Sayce, A.-H.
"Gleanings from the land of Egypt: 3. The Tomb of (Ahanakht) at Bersheh." *RecTrav.* 13 (1890), pp. 187–191.

Schenkel, W.
Frühmitteläqyptische Studien. Bonner orientalistische Studien. Bonn: Selbstverlag des Orientalischen Seminars der Universität Bonn, 1962.

Sharpe, Samuel
Egyptian Inscriptions from the British Museum and other sources. 2nd series. London: Moxon, 1837, 1855.

Silverman, David P.
The Tomb Chamber of Ḫsw the Elder. Part I: *Illustrations.* American Research Center in Egypt Reports 10. Winona Lake: Eisenbraun's, 1988.

———
"Textual Criticism in the Coffin Texts." In *Religion and Philosophy in Ancient Egypt*, pp. 29–53. Yale Egyptological Studies 3. Edited by William K. Simpson. New Haven: Yale University Press, 1989.

———
"A Spell from an Abbreviated Book of the Two Ways in a Tomb in the Western Delta," pp. 853–76. In *Studies in Egyptology presented to Miriam Lichtheim,* Vol. II. Edited by Sarah Israelit-Groll. Jerusalem: The Magnes Press, The Hebrew University, 1990.

Spanel, Donald
"Toward a Reassessment of the Herakleopolitan Period and the Eleventh Dynasty: The Date of the Djehutynakht-Family Coffins from Bersheh (B1Bo–B7Bo)," forthcoming.

Spiegelberg, Wilhelm
"Varia: Die Inschrift Amenophis' III zu el-Bersche." *RecTrav.* 26 (1904), pp. 151–152.

Terrace, Edward L.B.
Egyptian Paintings of the Middle Kingdom. London and New York: George Allen and Unwin Ltd. and Georges Braziller, 1968.

Walle, B. van de
La transmission des textes littéraires égyptiennes. Brussels: Fondation Egyptologique Reine Elisabeth, 1948.

Willems, Harco.
"The Nomarchs of the Hare Nome and Early Middle Kingdom History." *JEOL* 28 (1983–84), pp. 80–102.

———
Review of *Das Grab des ꜣInỉ-ỉtỉ.f,* Grabung im Asasif 1963–1970, Band V, by B. Jaroš-Deckert. *BiOr* 46 (1989), cols. 598–599.

Willems, Harco.
Chests of Life: A Study of the Typology and Conceptual Development of Middle Kingdom Standard Class Coffins. Mededelingen en verhandelingen van het Vooraziatisch-Egyptisch Genootschap "Ex Oriente Lux" 25. Leiden: Ex Oriente Lux, 1988.

———
"Deir el Bersheh: A Preliminary Report." *GM* 110 (1989), pp. 75–95.

Zimmer, T.
"La Moyenne Egypte: methodes d'investigation bibliographiques et priorités." *BSFE* 96 (1983), pp. 22–25.